THE BRITISH WAR IN AFGHANISTAN

'The best stories have been told a hundred times. They have been revisited by historians, adapted by novelists, travestied by film-makers, recycled by TV producers. None of those versions, however, can avoid the distorting wisdom of hindsight. For this reason if no other, the appearance of …[this] series of official reports … should be greeted with cries of joy.' *Financial Times*

'We congratulate you for the beauty and the value of the books shown.' Professor Dr Ionel Oprisan, *Editura Saeculum*, Romania, on *The Irish Book of Death and Flying Ships*

'A rare insight into the catastrophic Gallipoli campaign.' *Worcester Evening News* [on *Lord Kitchener and Winston Churchill*]

'There is a clarity that resonates down the years and it is because of this that [the books] have considerable appeal.… The events, although described in the cold official prose of senior military and political figures, nevertheless retain a freshness and immediacy.' *Worcester Evening News* [on *British Battles of World War I*]

'This is raw history.… To counter the polite but insistent letters of the British are translated speeches by the Führer, showing what his true intentions were. It's particularly satisfying to see Goering getting a dressing down from a British diplomat.' *Military Weekly* [on *War 1939*]

'This is inspired publishing, not only archivally valuable, but capable of bringing the past back to life without the usual filter of academic or biographer.' *Guardian*

'Intriguing insight into political background to conflict.' Customer review [on *War in the Falklands, 1982*]

'Tim Coates' brilliant new book … uses original FBI files to recreate the period.' *Daily Express* [on *John Lennon: the FBI files*]

'Congratulations … for unearthing and reissuing such an enjoyable vignette.' [on *Wilfred Blunt's Egyptian Garden*] *The Spectator*

'Like Samuel Pepys, Denning … took obvious pleasure in the English language. His canny, wry and at times indignant observations make this official report of a board of inquiry a wonderful entertaining and extraordinary read.… The writing is superb and the photojournalism is just as revealing.' *The Age* (Victoria, Australia) [on *The Scandal of Christine Keeler and John Profumo: Lord Denning's Report, 1963*]

'These volumes are monuments to the maligned bureaucratic architects who shaped our contemporary world – in part chilling, in part inspiring.… They show the search for order and sense amid the chaos of events, the debris of crime or the aftermath of disaster.' *Times Higher Education Supplement*

'Brilliant publishing to produce this useful edition within only 24 hours of the release of the report.' [on *The Hutton Report, 2003*] *The Bookseller*

'It is difficult to praise the idea, the format, the selection and the quality of the series too highly.' *Times Higher Education Supplement*

'Who, outside a few historians, knows that the British invaded Tibet? We approach these stories with an immediacy it would be impossible to contrive … from one of the richest unexplored attics in the country.' Robert Winder, *The Independent*

'This is raw history … An excellent series. It's particularly satisfying to see Goering getting a dressing down from a British diplomat.' [on *Dealing with Hitler*] *Military Illustrated*

'Very good to read … insight into important things … inexorably moving … If you want to read about the Titanic, you won't read a better thing … a revelation.' *Open Book*, BBC Radio 4

'The account is humane, moving and beautifully told. Each pocket-size edition tells a good story. This excellent series makes enjoyable reading. More please.' [on *Tragedy at Bethnal Green*] *Times Higher Education Supplement*

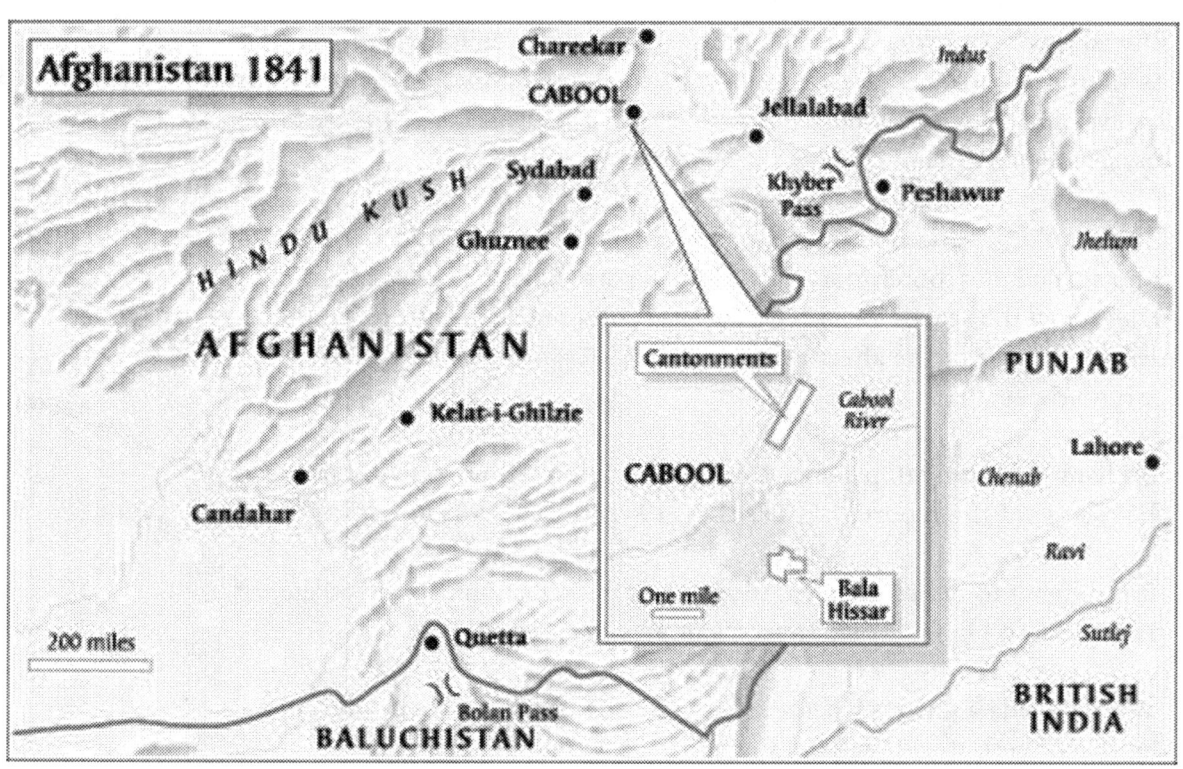

THE BRITISH WAR IN AFGHANISTAN

The Dreadful Retreat from Kabul in 1842

MOMENTS OF HISTORY
Series editor: Tim Coates

London and New York

© Tim Coates 2006

All rights reserved. No part of this publication may be reproduced, stored in a retrieval system, or transmitted in any form or by any means, electronic, mechanical, photocopying, recording or otherwise, without the permission of the publisher.

Applications for reproduction should be made in writing to Tim Coates,
c/o Littlehampton Book Services, Durrington, West Sussex BN13 3RB, UK

ISBN 1 84381 006 9

The material for the first part of this book is drawn from The Controller's Library of The Stationery Office in London. TSO have generously given access to the Library for the content of this series. First published by HMSO as *Papers Relating to Military Operations in Affghanistan. Presented to both Houses of Parliament, by Command of Her Majesty* (1843).
© Crown copyright
This selection and this edition © Tim Coates.

A CIP catalogue record for this book is available from the British Library.

Editor: Frances Baird
Keying: Tricia Lord
Maps: Duncan Stewart
Design: Sarah Theodosiou
Series Editor: Tim Coates

Cover photograph © Mary Evans Picture Library
The assassination of Sir Alexander Burnes, 2 November 1841
(by Richard Caton Woodville)

About the series

The books in this series are historic official papers which are made available in a popular form and are chosen for the quality of their story-telling. Some subjects are familiar but others are less well known. Each is a moment in history.

A complete list of titles is to be found at the back of this book. Further details are available on www.timcoatesbooks.com

About the series editor, Tim Coates

Tim Coates studied at University College, Oxford and at the University of Stirling. After working in the theatre for a number of years, he took up bookselling and became managing director, firstly of Sherratt and Hughes bookshops, and then of Waterstone's. He is known for his support for foreign literature, particularly from the Czech Republic and his work to improve the British Public Library Service. He specializes in the republishing of interesting archives. The idea for these books came while searching through the bookshelves of his late father-in-law, Air Commodore Patrick Cave OBE. Tim Coates is married to Bridget Cave, has two sons and lives in London. He is the author of *Patsy: The Story of Mary Cornwallis-West* (Bloomsbury 2003), the good library guide blog, www.goodlibraryguide.com/blog/ and "Delane's war", the story of the editor of *The Times* in the first year of the Crimean war.

Tim Coates welcomes views and ideas on the series. He can be e-mailed at timcoatesbooks@yahoo.com.

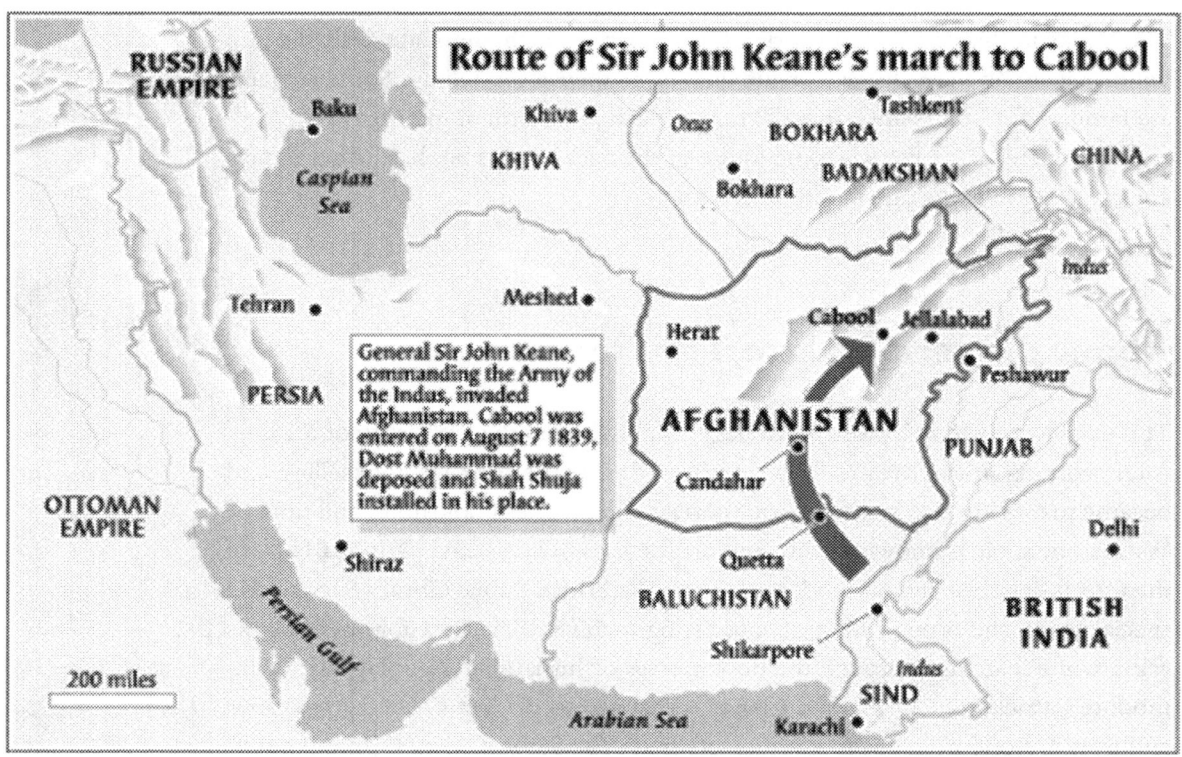

CONTENTS

Glossary xi

Introduction xiii

Papers Relating to Military Operations in Afghanistan 1

Extracts from the Diaries of Lieutenant Vincent Eyre and Lady Florentia Sale 67

Maps
    Afghanistan 1841 iv
    Route of Sir John Keane's march to Cabool viii
    Retreat from Cabool, 1842 2

The publishers would like to thank the following photographers and organizations for their kind permission to reproduce the photographs in this book. Every effort has been made to trace the holders of any copyright material. However, if there are any omissions we will be happy to rectify them in future editions.

© Mary Evans Picture Library, London – p. 15 (by A.D. McCormick) and p. 68 (by A.B.)

Illustrations on pp. xiv and 70 from the *The Afghan Wars*, 1830–1919 by T.A. Heathcote (Osprey 1980); on p. 113 from *Afghanistan* by Lt General Sir George MacMunn (1929)

GLOSSARY

Atchakzye One of the great Afghan tribes
Ameer Commander or chief; title assumed by Dost Muhammad Khan
Atta Ground wheat
Ayah Nurse
Bahadur Title of respect, often added to names of officers and officials
Bala Hissar Royal citadel; upper citadel
Barukzye One of the five great Dooranee tribes
Batta Allowance in addition to ordinary pay; subsistence money
Burj Tower
Chauki Watch-house; station
Chupatti Thin flat piece of unleavened bread
Chuprassie Uniformed office messenger or henchman
Cossid Running messenger
Dal Pigeon-pea; a purée of pulse
Dawk Mail-post
Doolie Litter; palanquin
Dooranee Name of five great tribes
Durbar Body of officials at an Indian court
Eusofzye Afghan tribe holding the territory north of Peshawur
Feringhee European
Firman Decree or judicial decision
Ghazee Champion of religion, a slayer of infidels
Ghee Clarified butter, especially made with milk from Asian buffalo
Ghilzie A great Afghan tribe
Godown Storehouse
Goorkha Native of Nepal
Jan-Baz Afghan horse
Jemadar Native officer in the Indian army, subordinate to a subahdar
Jezail Long rifle
Jezailchee Rifleman
Jirga Council of tribal leaders
Kafila Caravan, caravan train
Kajawa Camel litter for women; a kind of large pannier or wooden frame, a pair of which were carried by a camel

Khan Nobleman; in Kabul the title is assumed by everyone, even the lowest
Kotal Mountain pass
Kuzzilbash Descendant of the Persians, wearing a red cap
Lac 100,000 (of rupees); an indefinitely vast number
Munshi Interpreter or secretary
Naib Deputy
Naik Corporal in the Indian military
Nawab Prince
Nullah River or stream
Palkee Palanquin
Patan One of a race inhabiting Afghanistan and noted for courage and fierceness in ar
Posteen Afghan greatcoat, generally of sheepskin
Ressalah Squadron of native cavalry
Ressaldar Native captain in an Indian cavalry regiment
Ryot Peasant, or cultivating tenant
Seer Indian weight of widely ranging amount, officially about 2 lb
Sepoy Native soldier in the Indian army
Shroff Banker, money-lender
Sirdar Chief, military leader
Subahdar Native officer, corresponding to a captain
Syce Groom, mounted attendant
Wuzeer Vizier
Xummel Coarse blanket
Yaboo Afghan pony

In March 1839 the British Army in India, 'the Army of the Indus', entered Afghanistan with the intention of installing Shah Shuja in place of Dost Muhammad Khan as leader of the country and preventing Afghanistan coming under the control of either Persia or Russia. The invasion was not provoked by any action other than a strategic anxiety and was in conflict with the guidance of senior political advisers, who were inclined to work with Dost Muhammad rather than against him. Shah Shuja had previously been deposed by the Afghans on a number of occasions and could only maintain a regal position with the active support of the British Army.

The size of the army varies in different documents, for reasons that are connected to the story told in these papers, but it may well have comprised 5,000 officers, 10,000 private soldiers and 60,000 members of families, traders and camp followers. They ascended the Bolan Pass to Quetta and proclaimed Shah Shuja at Kandahar. They moved on to Kabul where the new king and his family and court occupied the Bala Hissar fortress, which stands on the mountain dominating Kabul. The army were left to billet in a cantonment which lay to the north of the city on the plain, vulnerable to attack from the high surrounding mountains.

For 18 months the regime maintained its hold on power, but a desire from both London and the authorities in India that the British Army should withdraw was impossible to satisfy. Shah Shuja had no authority without them and he was not popular; indeed he was disliked. Moreover the British Army, as an occupying force, did not behave with credit, and it caused resentment with its lavish lifestyle and particularly with the soldiers' attitude and behaviour toward local women.

In November 1841 Sir William Macnaghten, the senior officer and 'envoy', reduced his payments of what were effectively bribes to the leaders of particular factions, and this was the precipitation of the events described in this book. The first part provides extracts of the official government account of the events from October 1841 to January 1842, in the order they appeared in the original report; the second is extracted from diaries of two of the survivors – Lieutenant Vincent Eyre,[1] Bengal Artillery, and Lady Florentia Sale,[2] wife of Major-General Sir Robert Sale – both of whom were finally released in September 1842.

The British Army has rarely elsewhere experienced a defeat of the kind that occurred in January 1842.

1 *The Military Operations at Kabul, with a Journal of Imprisonment in Afghanistan* (London: Spottiswode & Co., 1843)
2 *Journal of Disasters in Afghanistan* (London: John Murray, 1843)

Dost Muhammad Khan, 'The Great Ameer' (1793–1863), reinstated after withdrawal of British in October 1941

Papers Relating to Military Operations in Afghanistan

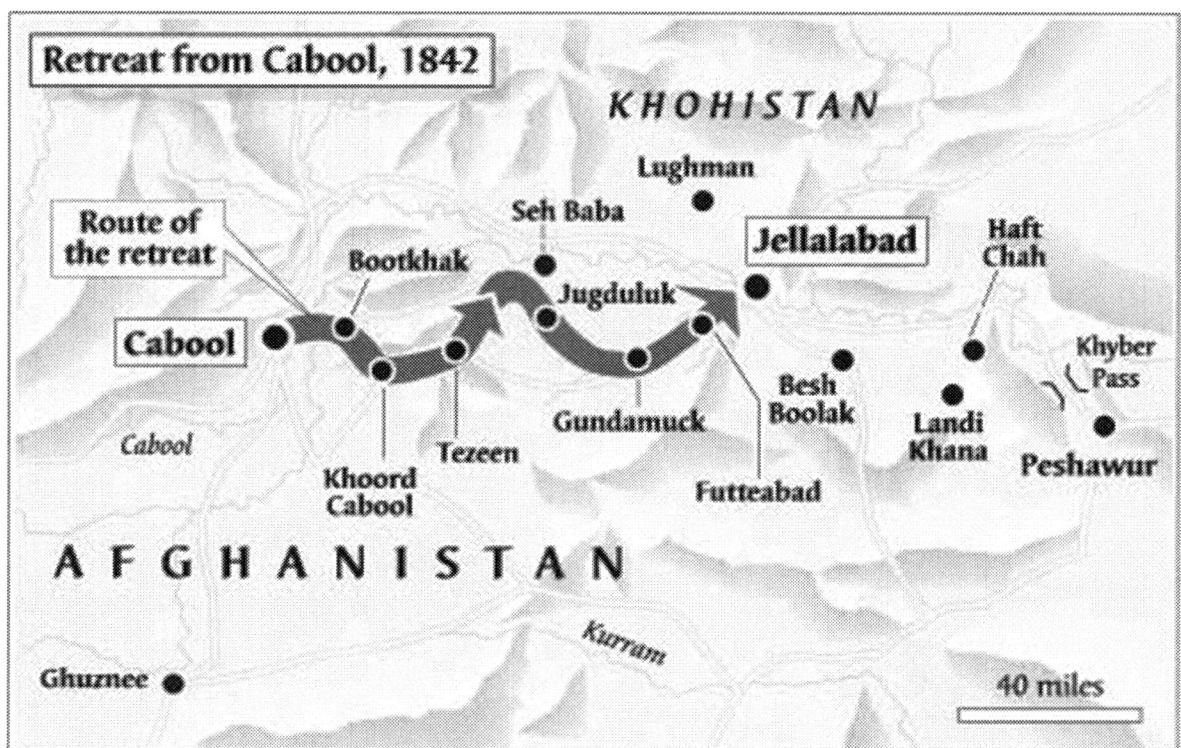

The Governor-General of India in Council to the Secret Committee of the East India Company

Fort William, December 22, No. 109, 1841

It may be of advantage to your Honourable Committee that we endeavour to draw out a succinct narrative of the disastrous events which have lately occurred at Cabool, and in other parts of Afghanistan, with some examination of the causes which have led to these events and an exposition of the views with which, in the present state of our information, we are disposed to regard them.

We are unfortunately able but most imperfectly to perform this task. We have before us but few authentic documents; the latest date of the dispatches received from Sir William Macnaghten is only of 26th October; and all else that we know is collected from two or three dispatches written, upon this side of the passes, by Sir Robert Sale, from fragments of private correspondence, and from the rumours which have reached Candahar and Peshawur. But we believe that the facts in our possession, such as we shall give them to your Honourable Committee, may be relied upon.

The force at, and near, Cabool consisted, at the beginning of October, of Her Majesty's 13th and 44th Regiments of Foot, the 5th, 35th, 37th and 54th Regiments Bengal Native Infantry, the 5th Bengal Light Cavalry, a company of foot and a troop of horse artillery, besides minor details, in addition to two regiments of the disciplined infantry of the Shah's contingent, the headquarters of one of the corps of Hindoostanee cavalry belonging to that contingent, a mountain train of artillery attached to the same force under Captain Backhouse, of the Bengal Army, and a number of the Shah's guns under the charge of Lieutenant Warburton, with some strength, of the extent of which we are not accurately informed, of Afghan horse, partly under British command.

Of this force it was intended that Her Majesty's 13th, and the 35th and 37th Native Infantry, with a company of artillery, some sappers, etc., should proceed in the autumn to the provinces; two native regiments, and, if it should be found necessary, one European regiment, the 9th, being held in readiness for their relief. One of the Shah's Hindoostanee regiments, the 6th, was stationed at Chareekar, about 130 miles to the north of Cabool, and the remainder of the force was divided between the Bala Hissar, which overlooks the town, and in which the Shah resides, and the cantonment, which is a strong post about three miles to its north.

The aspect of things at the capital, even to the very end of October, appears to have been altogether pacific. Many of our officers resided, some with their families, in the town. The commissariat establishments were partly placed within its walls; our officers are said to have walked and rode in all directions without apprehension or interruption; and, though it was notorious that the priesthood and the chiefs of clans, with a large portion of the military retainers immediately dependent upon them, regarded with extreme dislike the state of things introduced under our influence, no idea was entertained of a universal discontent, or of the hazard of a general and formidable outbreak. Indeed, for many weeks previously, almost every communication, public and private, had represented the country as improving, and the difficulties of our Afghan relations as in a fair train for permanent satisfactory settlement.

An expedition against a predatory tribe at Zao, in the direction of Ghuznee, had been undertaken at the end of September. It had terminated successfully, and without bloodshed, in the submission of the tribe. Our troops were on their return to Cabool, and 20th October had been named by Sir William Macnaghten as the day on which he should put Sir Alexander Burnes in charge of his office and set out on his journey to Bombay.

By a private letter from Sir W. Macnaghten, dated 6th October, we learnt that some discontent had exhibited itself on the part of several of the chiefs of the tribes of the eastern Ghilzies, who command the passes leading from Gundamuck, to within 12 or 13 miles of Cabool. These passes are of a very difficult character, but a good understanding had been maintained with the chiefs from our entrance into the country up to that time. The ground of this discontent was a reduction in the amount of the grain allowances granted to the chiefs, the portion of the allowances remaining being regarded as more valuable to them than their receipts in the time of Dost Muhammad Khan, in consequence of the high prices at present prevailing. It appears that, on this reduction being made, the chiefs left Cabool and an insurrection took place in the passes, the dawks were robbed and all regular communications were stopped. These disturbances were lightly treated; an Afghan chief, of supposed loyalty and influence, was sent forward to deal with the malcontents; and it was hoped that peace would be restored, rather by negotiation than by force of arms.

Towards the 12th it had been determined that the passes should be forced. Her Majesty's 13th, the 35th Native Infantry and, subsequently, the 37th Native Infantry, a squadron of the 5th Bengal Cavalry, and some other horse, with a portion of artillery, were allotted to this service and placed under the command of Brigadier Sale; and Captain Macgregor, the political agent at Jellalabad, was attached to it. The Khoord Cabool Pass, as may be seen by the official dispatches, was gallantly forced on the 12th, though with a loss to the British troops employed of from 30 to 40 men. A night attack was the next day repelled by the 35th Native Infantry, and the enemy's position at Tezeen was subsequently attacked on the 22nd, with success.

Captain Macgregor, unguarded, and Captain Paton visited the camp of the insurgents. He was kindly received by the chiefs, and he believed that he had made a satisfactory arrangement with them; but, though for some days afterwards the professions of the chiefs were invariably those of peace and of friendship, the attacks from the hills upon the detachment in its advance were unceasing, and it will be seen, by Sir Robert Sale's reports, with what difficulties, and with how severe a loss of men and baggage, he made good his advance, on 31st October, to the station of Gundamuck, where was Captain Burn with a strong detachment of mountaineer jezailchees, chiefly of the Afreedee or Khyber tribes.

Sir William Macnaghten's official report, the latest we have received from him upon any subject, under date 26th October, gives his view of the origin and progress of this quarrel with the eastern Ghilzies.

Sir Robert Sale had found it desirable to take on with him only the 13th and 35th, with artillery, cavalry and details, from Khoord Cabool. The 37th Native Infantry was ordered, in the first instance, to remain in position, with a view mainly to keep open the communication, and was, subsequently, on the outbreak of the insurrection in the city, called back to Cabool – a movement it was only able to effect with loss of baggage and men (5 killed and 15 wounded).

At Gundamuck Sir Robert Sale was in a position of some difficulty: his camel-men were deserting him; his ammunition was in great part expended; he was overhung by the enemy in the hills; the post was not a strong one; and it was distant from any support which could be afforded to him from Peshawur. He had received a summons to return to Cabool, to which he felt himself obliged to represent, in answer, that without means of carriage, with the enemy in force upon every point of his passage, and ill-provided as he was with ammunition, the absolute destruction of his brigade would be the certain result of the attempt. He determined, therefore, on the advice of a council of war, upon retiring upon Jellalabad and making a strong entrenchment at that place.

On 6th November he destroyed a fort of one of the insurgent chiefs, of whose flight in revolt from Cabool he had received intimation, and, upon the 11th, he marched to Jellalabad, leaving Gundamuck in charge of Captain Burn with his detachment of jezailchees and a corps of Jan-Baz horse. These troops became rapidly disordered. The Jan-Baz horse, and a large number of the Afreedee jezailchees, went over to the enemy or deserted to their homes. With such of the jezailchees as adhered to him Captain Burn retired also to Jellalabad, leaving, however, two guns and much baggage behind him.

Brigadier Sale found himself at Jellalabad, surrounded and attacked by all the armed population of the country. He had at first but six days' provision; his men were harassed and the defences of the place were exceedingly weak. The latest letters from him are of 27th November; he had attacked and dispersed the enemy and collected supplies for 30 days. Ammunition had been sent from Peshawur; but it is uncertain whether it had reached him. All the later reports, however, from this post are in a tone of laudable and increasing confidence. The enemy, after their first defeat, had not again ventured to assail it; we may look, we trust, with certainty to the security of this portion of our troops.

Captain Ferris, an officer commanding one of the Shah's irregular Afghan regiments, had been posted at Besh Boolak, between the Khyber Pass and Jellalabad, with a detachment of his corps. When the country became disorganized in consequence of our troops falling back to Jellalabad, his camp was attacked by numbers of the surrounding tribes, but his men, chiefly Eusofzye Patans, from the country subject to the Sikhs, fought bravely, and he was able to cut his way through the enemy and to make good his retreat, though compelled to abandon about 38,000 rupees of public treasure and all private property.

Mr Mackeson, a gentleman not in the regular service, had charge of the fort of Ali Musjid in the Khyber Pass with 150 men, also of the Eusofzye tribe; and the Khyberees, when the infection of alarm and disorder reached them, showed an inclination to disturb the peace of the pass. The chiefs disavowed all participation with the tribes in this feeling, but the fort was nevertheless attacked, and the enemy nearly crowned the heights; but the Eusofzyes were faithful and the assailants were repulsed. In the end, by the interference of General Avitabile and Captain Mackeson, the insurgents departed and the fort has been replenished. The known march of large Sikh and British reinforcements towards Peshawur, and the interest of the chiefs in keeping on terms with us, for the sake of their considerable pecuniary allowances, may, possibly, lead the Khyberees not to declare against us.

We know not with accuracy what indications of trouble preceded the tragical events which took place on 2nd November at Cabool. In the letter from Captain Mackeson at Peshawur of 11th October, forwarded to your Honourable Committee with our dispatch of the 20th ultimo, mention is made of six leading Dooranee chiefs having incurred the king's displeasure with reference to discontents, openly and disrespectfully evinced by them, in consequence of reductions in the allowances to which the narrowness of the king's finances led him, under Sir William Macnaghten's advice, to have recourse. We have received no official report regarding that occurrence, but your Honourable Committee is aware from the papers which we have at different times forwarded to you that a reduction of the retainers of the military khans, and the formation of bodies of horse, paid directly by the Crown, had been among the objects of policy which have appeared most important for giving strength and stability to the king's government.

Your Honourable Committee is sensible also that it has been a necessary and prominent object of our care to bring the Shah's disbursements, as nearly as possible, within the limit of his income. In pursuance of these objects, the six chiefs referred to appear to have been subject to some retrenchment, and opposition at one time seems to have been attempted, in an indirect manner, to the organization of the bodies of horse to be paid by the state. The Shah himself, who has made over for the most part the duty of administration to his minister, Mahomed Oosman Khan, an individual possessing the entire confidence and approbation of Sir William Macnaghten, may be believed to have thrown the responsibility of these distasteful measures mainly on that officer, with whom the envoy and minister was, doubtless, in general estimation, identified; and we find accordingly that, in the popular rumours which have prevailed, at least the dissatisfaction of the Shah with the state of things existing at Cabool has been very readily taken for granted.

From a précis of intelligence addressed by Lady to Sir Robert Sale, we learn that there was a succession of engagements from 2nd to 8th November, by which, though our troops invariably behaved well and obtained advantage, but little impression was made upon the enemy. We further know that a successful sally was made on the 13th, and that the stock of provisions, which on the 8th was estimated as only sufficient for five days, was, on the 14th, equal to ten days' consumption; and the tone in a note from Sir William Macnaghten to Captain Macgregor, at Jellalabad, of the 18th, was certainly not one of any immediate apprehension. Negotiations were still apparently open between Sir William Macnaghten and some of the chiefs, but, as far as is stated, with no satisfactory prospect.

We must necessarily regard the position of our force at that city with great anxiety. It was divided; its means of supply were narrow and precarious; the whole surrounding country was opposed to it; and the season was approaching at which the passes of the hills would be closed by the snow. On the other hand, here are bravery and discipline; the interval between the Bala Hissar and the cantonments is open and a junction could easily be made; and the town may be forced to afford supplies; whilst the falling of the snows may have the effect of forcing, at least, a partial dispersion of the enemy. We must painfully await the result, for it seems to be physically impossible that troops could, before the spring, approach Cabool for rescue.

We have thus stated, in as accurate an outline as the means at our command will permit, the afflicting events by which our position in Afghanistan has been so suddenly and seriously endangered. We have marked the obstinacy with which, notwithstanding the apparent accommodation of the eastern Ghilzie chiefs with Captain Macgregor about 22nd November, the tribes under them – stated not to be numerous or powerful, though in possession of a very difficult country – contested every portion of the advance of the British troops eastward at a time when these tribes stood alone openly committed to insurrection.

This discontent found ready material for the excitement of hostility and disorder in the national and religious feeling of the Afghan tribes, whom our presence, and the measures pursued under our influence, have failed to conciliate. The population – with the exception of the labouring cultivators, who probably regard our ascendancy with satisfaction, but whose goodwill is of little value in such a crisis – is armed and accustomed to turbulence and violence; and time has not admitted of any effectual repression of these habits, or of giving stability to the new order of things.

We have applied ourselves immediately to concerting such measures, and issuing such instructions, as the exigency of the case seemed to require and admit. We have laid it down as a rule of our conduct that we would do all in our power to rescue our detachments wherever they may be encompassed by danger; but that, if the position of command and influence, which we have held at the capital of Afghanistan, should once be absolutely and entirely lost, we would make no more sacrifices of the very serious and extensive nature which could alone be effectual for the re-establishment of our supremacy throughout the country, except under positive instructions from England.

If matters should, by force or negotiation, be restored at Cabool, we shall have time for deliberation; and if they should be but rarely maintained in their present state of precarious difficulty, we must await the approach of spring before we can act with vigour or advantage. We have particularly, however, felt it our duty distinctly at this distance to give instructions applicable to all contingencies, and therefore to contemplate the most unfavourable issue to the struggle which our troops are maintaining at Cabool; and, in this case, upon the anticipation of which we cannot conceal from ourselves the hazard of extending dangers, and of the insurrection assuming in other quarters also the same national and united character, we have authorized General Nott and Major Rawlinson – with such caution and deliberation in their military and political proceedings as may serve to avoid discredit and to promise safety – so to shape their course as best to promote the end of the eventual relinquishment of our direct control in the several Afghan provinces, and to provide for the concentration of all forces and detachments as may be most conducive to the security of the troops.

On our side, we would immediately collect a strong force at Peshawur, with the view of its acting in aid of Sir Robert Sale at Jellalabad and making a demonstration of strength on that frontier; and the troops as here enumerated are already on their march, viz., 60th, 64th, 30th and 53rd Regiments Native Infantry, with details of cavalry, and a company of European foot artillery. Two other regiments, one of them Her Majesty's 9th Foot, are held also in readiness to march in the event of Mr Clerk and the commander-in-chief so determining; and a Sikh detachment, consisting of four battalions of infantry, 2,000 horse and artillery, has been directed by the Lahore durbar to act in co-operation with it. We hope that this force will be sufficient to keep in awe the tribes of the Khyber Pass, or, if necessary, to force that defile and give support to General Sale and, ultimately, should circumstances admit of such course, to form a base from whence communications may be opened with Cabool. We have requested the government of Bombay, and Major Outram, to detain, for the present, all the troops which are present in Upper Sinde, and in any event to look to his having a force of not less than two effective brigades at Sukkur and Shikarpore.

We feel it to be absolutely necessary that we thus hold a strong front upon the line of the Indus. And this front it is our intention and determination, subject to the orders of your Honourable Committee, firmly to maintain; and we have endeavoured to do this without in any degree relaxing from that care which is due to the protection of our frontiers, and to the preservation of tranquillity in the territories of India and in those of our dependent allies. Even if six regiments should be sent to Peshawur, the state of our northern cantonments will be such as to enable his excellency the commander-in-chief to collect for the field, at a very short notice and in addition to an ample force of artillery, an army of not less than 12 or 14 regiments of infantry and nine or ten of cavalry, of which at least three of the former and two of the latter would be Europeans. For details of the orders which we have given, and of the discretion which we have requested his excellency the commander-in-chief, in communicating with Mr Clerk, to exercise, we would refer your Honourable Committee to the copies of our several dispatches, the purport and effect of which will, we trust, meet with your approbation, particularly in the part of them which relates to using the occasion in order to establish more intimately our union with the Sikh government.

AUCKLAND
W.W. BIRD
WM CASEMENT
H.T. PRINSEP

Sir W.H. Macnaghten, Bart, Envoy and Minister at the Court of Shah Shuja, to T.H. Maddock, Esq., Secretary to the Government of India

Cabool, October 26, 1841

I have now the honour to report the circumstances attending the recent rebellion of certain of the eastern Ghilzie chiefs. The first intimation I received of this rebellion was about three weeks ago, to the effect that the chiefs had suddenly left Cabool; and the day after I learnt that they had stopped a caravan on the high road and had taken the property and its owners to the hills at a distance from the road.

I immediately waited upon his majesty, and prevailed upon him to send the governor, Humza Khan, with a message to the rebels, inviting them to return to their allegiance and promising redress of any real grievance they might have sustained. This mission failed of success because Humza Khan was the chief instigator of the rebellion.

Two reasons have been assigned for this rebellion. First, the reduction of the allowances of the Ghilzie chiefs; and, secondly, the engagement that was required of them to be responsible for robberies by the eastern Ghilzies, wherever committed.

On the first point I may observe that the necessities of his majesty, and the frequent prohibitions I had received against further reliance on the resources of the British government, appeared to admit of no alternative. I was assured that the chiefs had admitted the justice of, and cheerfully acquiesced in, the reduction; moreover that, after the reduction was effected, the chiefs would, in consequence of the enhanced value of grain, receive larger allowances than they did in the time of Dost Muhammad.

On the second point I am compelled to state that the grievance of the chiefs was well founded. Their liabilities should have been only co-extensive with their respective jurisdictions. Unfortunately they never represented their grievance to me. They have been prohibited from visiting me on the part of the Shah by the before-named governor, a worthless man, alike inimical to us and to his majesty. The good result of the recent rebellion is the disgrace and imprisonment of this man. His father was killed in the Shah's service; and his majesty, in an amiable weakness, was unwilling to acknowledge the demerits of the son, of which, however, he is now fully sensible.

One of the chief rebels, Mahomed Shah Khan, has very large possessions in the district of Lughman. I therefore urged the minister to send out a relative of his own with 300 Huzarbash horse to that neighbourhood. This was done without the delay of an hour, and the designs of the rebels were for the time frustrated. They attacked the party en route but did comparatively little damage; and the conspirators found it necessary to separate, and each to look after his individual interests, before the plot was matured.

There are four thanas, or posts, guarded by Ghilzies, between Cabool and

Gundamuck. The first belongs to a chief named Khoda Buksh, a relative by marriage of the ex-Ameer Dost Muhammad Khan; the second to Sher Mahomed Khan; the third to Allahzar Khan; and the fourth to Gool Mahomed Khan. The second named of these (who has by far the greatest influence) was gained over to our cause at an early period, and the third was always staunch in his allegiance. Khoda Buksh and Gool Mahomed went into open rebellion, and with them was joined Mahomed Shah Khan, a Ghilzie chief with extensive property in Lughman, and a relative also, by marriage, of the ex-Ameer.

The conduct of Gool Mahomed was the most inexcusable of all. On the Shah's arrival in this country, that individual was in a state of destitution and was placed in power and affluence by his majesty. He has been indefatigable in his endeavours to stir up the surrounding tribes to rebellion, but I have much gratification in adding that he has in no one instance succeeded, a fact which speaks well for his majesty's government. Gool Mahomed Khan was immediately deposed, and his place supplied by Burkut Khan, a chief of great influence and respectability.

On the separation of the rebels, Mahomed Shah Khan retreated to Lughman. Khoda Buksh Khan, with not more than 100 followers, proceeded to occupy the Khoord Cabool Pass; and Gool Mahomed Khan went into his own country to raise the tribes. Lughman was already occupied by the Huzarbash horse, and I had no apprehension from that quarter. I had the greatest confidence in the new chief appointed by his majesty to supersede Gool Mahomed, and the first thing to be done was to dislodge Khoda Buksh and his party of rebels from the strong defile which they had occupied. The manner in which this service was performed has doubtless been reported to government by Major-General Elphinstone, CB, and it only remains for me to add that the prowess displayed by the British troops on this occasion was the admiration of all the Afghans, and there were not a few on our side who witnessed it.

Captain Macgregor having in the meantime returned from the Zoormut expedition, I caused him to communicate with the rebels, and he promised, in his majesty's name and my own, to inquire into, and redress, all their grievances. Messengers with conciliatory proposals were also sent, but to no purpose. Whilst professing the greatest desire to return to their allegiance, the party of Khoda Buksh and Gool Mahomed (the latter had joined the former after his expulsion from the pass) made a night attack on the position of the 35th Regiment of Native Infantry at Khoord Cabool, the particulars of which also have no doubt been communicated to the government.

On this occasion a party of His Majesty's Own Afghan Horse were present in our camp; and rumours, I understand, are rife that this party (consisting of about 80 persons) were guilty of treachery and actually fired upon our troops. The particulars of the case have not yet reached me, but it shall be duly inquired into, and his majesty will, I feel assured, make a signal example of anyone who may be proved to have thus offended. But if this party of Afghans suffered themselves to be surprised by a night attack, or even if, in the confusion of the moment, they fired shots in the direction of our own camp, it would be uncharitable in anyone familiar with the Afghan character to form from such premises the conclusion that they were guilty of deliberate treachery. But I merely wish his lordship in council to suspend his judgement on this transaction, for I well know the predisposition that exists in certain quarters to condemn, without hesitation and without reason, every Afghan institution, and that even the irreproachable character of his majesty has not secured him from the attacks of malevolence and calumny.

I have now received information from Captain Macgregor to the effect that our differences with the chiefs have been amicably arranged. The particulars have not reached me; but when Captain Macgregor submits a statement of his negotiations, a copy of it shall be forwarded without loss of time for the information of government. From what little I know of the terms conceded to the rebels, they would seem to me to be too favourable; but I have the fullest reliance on Captain Macgregor's discretion. The chiefs have furnished hostages and have consented to the appointment of Burkut Khan, by which means their confederacy has been dissolved.

I have been thus particular in detailing the circumstances of this rebellion from my conviction that the most false and exaggerated reports regarding it will be circulated by a class of persons whom I have already described to his lordship in council, and whose sole pursuit is the dissemination of groundless and alarming reports through the medium of the public prints.

The inconvenience to which we have been subjected by the interruption of our communications has been very great, but it only shows how easily annoyance may be inflicted, by means which would otherwise be contemptible, on a government which has so long a line of mountainous country to defend and whose chiefs have been so accustomed to a life of lawless turbulence that they do not hesitate to array themselves in opposition to authority, upon the slightest provocation and without a hope of ultimate success.

We have learned, by the experience of this rebellion, one important fact, which is that our regular European and Hindoostanee troops fight against Afghans, in their native hills, to a great disadvantage. The superior agility of the latter enables them to evade pursuit, and their fuzils, or long guns, carry with deadly precision to a distance where our muskets are harmless. There is now no enemy to oppose us in the open plain, and should we hereafter be forced into hostilities the desultory mountain warfare will doubtless be that with which we shall have to contend.

Should his lordship in council therefore resolve on increasing his majesty's force, with a view of recalling the regular regiments from this country, I would suggest that, instead of organizing any more Hindoostanee troops, three infantry corps should be raised from the Eusofzyes, Suhaks, Undurees, Kohistanees, Khyberees and the inhabitants of other mountainous regions, to undergo a moderate degree of discipline and to be armed with the jezail of the country. By a judicious admixture of different tribes, by attention to their prejudices and by regular pay, I should have little fear of their fidelity. In the meantime endeavours will be made to impart as great a degree of efficiency as possible to his majesty's jezailchees, who are a very useful body of men. In the above opinion I am supported by the authority of Major-General Elphinstone, CB, of Lieutenant-Colonel Sir A. Burnes, CB, and of Brigadier Anquetil.

It is my intention to forward a copy of this letter, for the information of the honourable the secret committee, through the government of Bombay.

W.H. MACNAGHTEN
Envoy and Minister

Major-General Sir Robert Sale to Captain Grant

Camp, Bootkhak, October 12, 1841

I have the honour to state to you, for the information of Major-General Elphinstone, CB, that the task of forcing the pass of Khoord Cabool and defeating the rebels posted within it has, this morning, been accomplished.

After fully weighing the whole of the information brought to me at various periods in the course of yesterday, I came to the conclusion that the main body of the insurgents was posted behind a breastwork near the middle of the pass, and that they would defend it as well as the almost inaccessible heights on either flank of it.

My plan of attack was therefore arranged as follows. I determined to employ 200 jezailchees, under the well-known sirdar, Jan Fishan Khan, to create a diversion by assaulting, in flank and rear, the precipitous ridge which forms the southern side of the Durra, whilst the troops under my command entered its gorge and attacked the enemy in front. The force left camp at 6 a.m. The advanced guard consisted of the two guns of foot artillery, under Lieutenant Dawes, two companies of the 13th Light Infantry, under Captain Fenwick and Lieutenant George King, the flank companies of the 35th Native Infantry under Captain Younghusband and a detachment of pioneers under Captain

Broadfoot, the whole being in charge of Captain Seaton, 35th Regiment of Native Infantry. The remainder of the 13th and 35th formed our main body.

As we approached the insurgents' position, we found that the reports of our spies had been substantially correct, but that the enemy were withdrawing from behind their breastwork in the valley and occupying the rocky ridges of the mountains on either side. They opened upon us a well-directed fire and, at the very commencement of the affair, I received a wound from a ball, above the ankle, which ultimately compelled me to leave the field.

Whilst I remained on it, however, I directed two companies of the 13th and one of the 35th to ascend the precipices on either hand in face of the enemy, and I must, in justice to them, mention the gallantry, activity and perseverance with which this duty was performed and the enemy driven by our skirmishers from point to point of eminences almost perpendicular. When compelled to retire, I resigned the command into the hands of Lieutenant-Colonel Dennie, CB, and have the pleasure to forward his report detailing the further progress and completion of the affair.

I beg to add that, whilst I remained at the head of the force, the conduct of both officers and men afforded me the highest satisfaction, and I am greatly pleased with the spirited and judicious manner in which Lieutenant-Colonel Dennie brought the matter to a close.

The exertions of my brigade-major, Captain Wade, and of Captain Havelock and Lieutenant Airey of Major-General Elphinstone's personal staff, who attached themselves to me as volunteers on this service, demand my amplest acknowledgements. The last-mentioned of these officers had a horse shot under him. I beg to forward the casualty return of the 13th; that of the artillery, sappers and 35th Native Infantry shall follow.

I am thankful for the promised reinforcement of two guns; and if the 37th Regiment Native Infantry can also be promptly sent out, it will relieve the troops from part of a very harassing outpost duty, in an exposed plain in the vicinity of mountains.

R. SALE

PS I ought not to have forgotten to mention that Captain Bellew, Assistant Quartermaster-General, who had previously, under General Elphinstone's instructions, reconnoitred the passes occupied by the enemy, accompanied me during my march from Cabool and ably aided me until the moment of my being wounded, upon which he continued to render valuable assistance to Lieutenant-Colonel Dennie. To Brevet-Captain Trevor, 3rd Light Cavalry, politically employed on this occasion, I was indebted for the information obtained at Bootkhak. Upon it my plan

Retreat from Cabool, 1842

of attack was based, and it proved correct in every particular; and he was personally active and conspicuous throughout the engagement.

Lieutenant-Colonel W.H. Dennie to Major-General Sir R.H. Sale

Camp, Bootkhak, October 12, 1841

I beg, on my return to camp, to report the detail of the progress and completion of the affair with the rebels, in the Khoord Cabool Pass, begun in so spirited a manner under your personal command this morning.

On receiving over charge of the troops, in consequence of your wound compelling you to leave the valley, I pursued your plan of operations by pressing the enemy on both flanks, as much as the nature of the ground would admit, and rapidly moving on the main column and guns, with the intention of dislodging them from their breast-works, if still occupied; but this the insurgents had evacuated, though they ventured to dispute the possession of the precipitous heights and to direct a well-aimed fire against our main force. Disconcerted, however, by the bold manner in which they were met by our skirmishers as they scaled the mountain sides, and by the steady progress of the advance, they gradually abandoned their first position and retired to the highest ridges and pinnacles of the Durra.

I had resolved, from the first, not to allow any lateral oppos-ition to divert me from the main purpose of clearing the valley, and a little after 7 a.m. I had the satisfaction of reaching the southern gorge of the pass and establishing there the 35th Native Infantry and the guns in an excellent post, constituted by the walls of a strong and capacious, though deserted, fort. By this time our skirmishers had everywhere got possession of the heights, and the Afghan force under Jan Fishan Khan had also crowned the mountains and displayed their banners on its summit.

You are aware that it was part of your original plan that the 13th Light Infantry should return to their encampment at Bootkhak. As the column marched back, the enemy again showed themselves on several points of the defile and opened a fire, and some loss was sustained in repelling these attacks and in withdrawing our flanking parties. The troops finally arrived at Bootkhak about 2 p.m., a good deal harassed by the exertions of the morning. You will see by the returns that the casualties have not been few, which arose from the great advantage afforded by the ground to an enemy trained to mountain warfare.

Permit me to add the expression of my admiration of the fearless manner in which the men of the 13th, chiefly young soldiers, ascended heights nearly perpendicular under the sharp fire of the insurgents. The sepoys of the 35th rivalled and equalled them in steadiness, activity and intrepidity. I am happy to say that no loss whatever of the baggage of the native infantry was sustained in traversing this valley of plunderers.

I have not yet received the casualty return of the 35th Regiment Native Infantry, but I have reason to believe that it is in amount about equal to that of the 13th, and I am informed that they have one officer, Captain Younghusband, severely wounded.

W.H. DENNIE

Return of killed, wounded and missing of the force under the command of Major-General Sir R.H. Sale, in forcing the Pass of Khoord Cabool on the 12th October 1841

2nd Company 6th Battalion Artillery 1 private, 3 horses wounded

Her Majesty's 13th Light Infantry 2 privates killed; 2 subalterns, 2 sergeants, 16 privates wounded

35th Regiment Native Infantry 2 privates killed; 1 captain, 1 naik, 8 sepoys wounded

Sappers and Miners 2 privates killed; 2 privates wounded

Total 6 privates killed; 1 captain, 2 subalterns, 2 sergeants, 1 corporal, 27 privates, 3 horses wounded

Grand total 6 killed; 33 wounded and 3 horses wounded

Names of officers wounded

General staff Major-General Sir R. Sale, KCB, commanding, severely; Captain Wade, major of brigade, slightly

13th Light Infantry Lieutenant Mein, severely; Ensign Oakes, slightly

35th Regiment Native Infantry Captain Younghusband severely

H. WADE
Major of Brigade

Major-General Sir R. Sale to Captain Grant

Camp in the Valley near Tezeen, October 23, 1841

I beg to acquaint you for the information of Major-General Elphinstone, CB, that the force united under my command, consisting of the 1st Brigade of Infantry, No. 6 Light Field Battery, the Mountain Train, the Corps of Sappers and Miners, a squadron of the 5th Light Cavalry and a ressalah of the Shah's 2nd Cavalry, marched from Khoord

Cabool towards Tezeen yesterday morning. Lieutenant-Colonel Monteath, 35th, commanded the advanced guard, Lieutenant-Colonel Dennie, 13th, the main column and Captain Oldfield, 5th Light Cavalry, the rearguard, in each of which troops of the several arms were appointed according to the best of my judgement.

The force felt its way cautiously through the defiles of the Huft Kotool, occupying with skirmishers the hills on either flank, and leaving parties for the protection of our baggage and rear on selected points. Nothing was seen of the enemy until the advance and main body had halted in the valley of Tezeen. From this low ground another vale stretches out towards the south-east, and on the sides and summits of the mountains which enclose the latter were posted in every quarter bodies of the insurgents, whilst another portion of their force, consisting of foot, led on by sirdars on horseback and their mounted followers, showed a determination to dispute with us the possession of a conical hill which partly closes the entrance of the branching valley and barred our approach to Mohamed Ufzal's fort, a large work backed by gardens which the rebels still garrisoned. From this eminence the advanced guard under Colonel Monteath drove them by a combined attack, and I then directed the 13th Light Infantry and a portion of Captain Abbott's battery to advance under Lieutenant-Colonel Dennie and assault the fort itself. The insurgents, however, abandoned it after directing from it a feeble fire.

I immediately determined to establish in the fort a depot for my sick and wounded, and to take it as a point of support for ulterior operations and an appui to my camp. But as the enemy continued to occupy in force a nearly circular range of heights, and even boldly to skirmish in a lower part of the valley, it became necessary to drive them from such segments of the mountain as would, if remaining in their hands, have given them the power to command our position and fire upon the troops with advantage at night. This led to a succession of skirmishes, which were maintained with great coolness and spirit by several companies of the 13th and one of the 35th, aided by the guns of Captain Abbott's battery and the Mountain Train and supported by the cavalry.

The combat was prolonged until after dusk and, the ammunition of one of the companies of the 13th having been expended, the company was compelled temporarily to retire and a very promising officer, Lieutenant Edward King, was killed at its head. A supply of cartridges and a reinforcement were promptly sent up, and the affair ended by the rebels being pushed off every part of the steep mountains which we designed to retain.

The returns will show that our loss has been slight, and I have no doubt that the enemy suffered severely from the fire of our skirmishers and the shot of our batteries. The force bivouacked in position without an attempt being made upon our line. Morning showed us the heights everywhere deserted by the rebels, and if a negotiation, which they have opened in very humble terms, should not end in their entire submission, I purpose to attack their principal fort tomorrow.

I regret to have to add, though every precaution was adopted for the security of our line of communication, a large interval was created between our main body and rear-guard by the circumstance of the latter having to await at Khoord Cabool the arrival of carriage from the capital for part of the public baggage. A light armed enemy, well acquainted with the country, did not fail to take advantage of this, and I fear that some ammunition and valuable stores have fallen into their hands. I beg to forward the returns of killed and wounded and of ammunition expended.

R. SALE

Return of the killed, wounded and missing of the force under the command of Major-General Sir R.H. Sale, in the attack on the enemy's position in the valley of Tezeen on the 22nd October 1841

2nd Company 6th Battalion Artillery 1 sergeant, 1 horse wounded

Squadron, 5th Light Cavalry 1 horse killed; 1 private wounded

Her Majesty's 13th Light Infantry 1 lieutenant, 3 privates killed; 1 lieutenant, 1 corporal, 7 privates wounded

Sappers and Miners 1 private killed; 1 lieutenant, 5 privates, 1 mule wounded

Mountain Train 2 privates wounded

Total 1 lieutenant, 4 privates, 1 horse killed; 2 lieutenants, 1 sergeant, 1 corporal, 15 privates, 1 horse, 1 mule wounded

Names of officers killed and wounded

Killed Lieutenant Edward King, Her Majesty's 13th Light Infantry

Wounded Lieutenant Frere, Her Majesty's 13th Light Infantry, slightly; Lieutenant Orr, Sappers and Miners, severely

H. WADE
Major of Brigade

Major-General Sir R. Sale to Captain Grant

Camp, Jugduluk, October 28, 1841

I have the honour to acquaint you, for the information of Major-General Elphinstone, CB, that the force under my command reached this place today; last night passed over without the slightest insult to our outposts at Kuttah Sung, but during the morning's march we descried small parties at a distance on both flanks, especially near the outlet of the Puree Durree, which afterwards united in a combined attack on our rearguard. Our loss has been small, and the enemy was everywhere baffled and held in check by the fire from our guns and skirmishers. Owing, however, to the jaded state of our camels, it became necessary to destroy a good deal of camp equipage to prevent its falling into the rebels' hands.

The daily repetition of these attacks has given rise to suspicions of the sincerity of the chiefs, in the mind of the political assistant, in which I am compelled to participate, though I shall be happy to find that their submission at Tezeen was made in good faith, and that these petty hostilities are the acts of men not under their control.

R. SALE

Major-General Sir R. Sale to Captain Grant

Camp, Gundamuck, October 30, 1841

Yesterday the force under my command was again engaged with the insurgents of these mountains, and the affair was the sharpest which we have had since penetrating the pass of Khoord Cabool. I experienced little molestation in my camp at Jugduluk, but observed, towards sunset and by moonlight, evident indications of the enemy, which had attacked our rearguard earlier in the day, being in the act of moving off over the hills with a view of concentrating between my force and Sookhab. Major-General Elphinstone is acquainted with the localities and will not have forgotten that the only entrance to the valley at Jugduluk, from the eastward, is by a long and winding kotal, overlooked and commanded by a lofty range of mountains, partially clothed with bushes and dwarf trees.

Of these really terrific eminences the rebels had, as I had anticipated, taken possession, but in more considerable numbers than we have been opposed to since leaving Tezeen. Holding all the salient points of the hills, and secured by breastworks, they showed a determination to dispute with the utmost obstinacy the progress of our flanking parties, and to endeavour to prevent the debouche of our advance and main column.

To enable us to effect this I had to detach companies from every corps in the force to the right and left and, aided by the artillery, they won their way inch by inch up the lofty heights. Much, however, remained to be done, and the fire of the mountaineers from several of the tallest summits was unabated. Success was everywhere doubtful, when a single company of the 13th, under Captain Wilkinson, was directed to advance up the defile itself. It pressed forward at a rapid pace, supported by all the reserves which remained available, and to the surprise of the whole force found that the enemy had neglected to guard the main outlet. This vanguard, therefore, its supports and the guns were quickly established on the narrow tableland, from which they had it in their power to take the whole of the defences of the rebels in reverse. Our troops commanded the route to Sookhab, and the enemy seemed to decline all further opposition.

The march was resumed; but as the cumbrous train of baggage filed over the mountain, the insurgents again appeared from beyond the most distant ridges and renewed the contest with increased numbers and the most savage fury. Our rearguard made the best dispositions for defence and rescue; but the suddenness of the onset caused some confusion, during which, notwithstanding the efforts of the troops, some baggage and camp equipage fell into the hands of their opponents. Captain Wyndham, of the 35th, was killed at this crisis of the affair; and several brave men of all the corps fell or were wounded. Soon, however, by the praiseworthy exertions and cool and soldier-like order and example of Captains Backhouse, Broadfoot and Fenwick, confidence was restored, the aspect of the affair changed and the rearguard extricated from the defile. It continued in the best order to retreat and to repel the enemy, who had followed it up to the point at which the loftier hills wear away.

Our casualties of yesterday and the day before amount to 130; amongst whom are one officer killed and four wounded. This loss will not be considered heavy by those who have seen the heights from which the rebels were driven and are acquainted with the habits and character of the mountaineers to whom we were opposed. I have today marched to this place without any interruption worthy of mention.

From the details of this dispatch the major-general commanding in Afghanistan will be enabled to draw his own inferences as to the actual state of our relations with the refractory chiefs who were admitted at Tezeen into a treaty of reconciliation with the government against which they had rebelled. But it belongs more peculiarly to my vocation in the field, now that there's a prospect of brief repose in the vicinity of this cantonment, to report with much satisfaction the cheerfulness, steadiness and perseverance with which the troops have performed every duty required of them. Since leaving Cabool they have been kept constantly on the alert by attacks by night and day; from the time of their arrival at Tezeen they have invariably bivouacked, and the safety of our positions has only been secured by unremitting labour, throwing up entrenchments and very severe outpost duty. Each succeeding morning has brought its affair with a bold and active enemy, eminently skilful in the species of warfare to which their attempts have been confined, and armed with jezails which have enabled them to annoy us at a range at which they could only be reached by our artillery. Though compelled by the effects of my late wound to witness these conflicts from a doolie, I must bear my equivocal testimony to the gallantry of officers and men on every occasion of contact with the enemy, and especially in scaling the tremendous heights above Jugduluk. I incise a casualty return.

I beg to express my sense of the highly able assistance which I have received in all our attacks and skirmishes, and throughout the operations, from Lieutenant-Colonels Dennie and Monteath, CB. I have been much pleased with the address and able management of Captain Abbott, of the artillery, who has twice commanded the advanced guard; and the exertions of Captain Wade, my brigade-major, and Captain Havelock, Persian interpreter to General Elphinstone (temporarily attached to me) in conveying my orders from point to point and aiding in the dispositions, deserve my warmest commendations.

R. SALE

Return of killed, wounded and missing of the force under the command of Major-General Sir Robert H. Sale on the advance to, and storming of, the Pass of Jugduluk, on 28th and 29th October, 1841

2nd Company 6th Battalion Artillery 1 private killed; 5 privates, 2 horses wounded

5th Regiment Light Cavalry Squadron 2 horses killed; 1 private, 2 horses wounded

Her Majesty's 13th Light Infantry 4 privates killed; 3 lieutenants, 30 privates wounded

35th Regiment Native Infantry 1 captain, 2 lieutenants, 2 subahdars, 1 jemadar, 1 corporal, 12 privates killed; 1 lieutenant, 1 jemadar, 4 sergeants, 1 corporal, 25 privates wounded

Sappers and Miners 1 sergeant, 6 privates killed; 1 subahdar, 1 jemadar, 4 sergeants, 1 corporal, 13 privates wounded

2nd Regiment Shah Shuja's Cavalry 1 horse wounded

Total 1 captain, 2 lieutenants, 2 subahdars, 1 jemadar, 1 sergeant, 1 corporal, 23 privates, 2 horses killed; 4 lieutenants, 1 subahdar, 2 jemadars, 8 sergeants, 2 corporals, 74 privates, 5 horses wounded

Names of officers killed and wounded

Killed Captain Wyndham, 35th Regiment Native Infantry

Wounded Lieutenant Jennings, 13th Light Infantry, severely; Lieutenant Holcombe, 13th Light Infantry, severely; Lieutenant Combe, 35th Native Infantry, severely

Captain Paton to Major-General Nott, Commanding at Candahar

Cabool, November 3, 1841

I have the honour, by direction of Major-General Elphinstone, commanding in Afghanistan, to request you will immediately direct the whole of the troops under orders to return to Hindoostan from Candahar to move upon Cabool, instead of Shikarpore, except any that shall have got beyond the Kojjuck Pass, and that you will instruct the officer who may command to use the utmost practicable expedition. You are requested to attach a troop of his majesty the Shah's Horse Artillery to the above force, and likewise half the 1st Regiment of Cavalry.

J. PATON
Assistant Quartermaster-General

Captain Mackeson, Political Agent at Peshawur, to Captain Lawrence, Assistant Governor-General's Agent, Ferozepore

Peshawur, November 9, 1841

I have the honour to enclose a copy of a letter, this instant received, from Captain Burn, dated Gundamuck, 5th November, and with reference to its contents have to request that you will communicate with the military authorities at Ferozepore, and urge on them the necessity of hastening, by every means in their power, the dispatch of the brigade warned for the Cabool relief.

I doubt the correctness of the report Captain Burn has received – of our troops being shut up in the Bala Hissar – and yet there must be some cause for the absence of all letters from the envoy; under any circumstances, the state of the country, owing to the rebellion among the eastern Ghilzies, is such as to make it highly desirable that the brigade destined for Afghanistan should arrive here as expeditiously as possible, consistent with a due regard to preserving its efficiency for work when it does arrive.

F. MACKESON

Major-General Sir Robert Sale to Captain Mackeson

Camp, Futteabad, November 11, 1841

In the course of my operations against the eastern Ghilzies, undertaken in pursuance of instructions from Major-General Elphinstone, I reached Gundamuck on the 30th ultimo and whilst there was made aware of the critical position in which the force of Cabool is placed, by the occupation of the city and of the heights around it by bodies of insurgents who have captured, it is said, one magazine and seem to have it in their power, now at the approach of winter, to cut off every supply from the troops in the Bala Hissar and entrenched cantonment.

I was unable as they and I had desired to march to their relief, partly in consequence of the desertion, in great numbers, of the owners of our hired carriage with their animals, and partly from our want of ammunition, half of our supply having been expended in our numerous affairs with the enemy, Jellalabad being at the same time menaced on the side of Lughman. I have determined to secure that important point by falling back upon it, and I hope to reach it tomorrow.

The commissariat officer will probably communicate with you on the subject of any wants he may have in that department; and I have now urgently to request the favour of your exerting your influence with the Sikh authorities at Peshawur to obtain for me, without delay, 200,000 rounds of musket ammunition, or, if that amount be not in readiness in their arsenal made up into cartridges, the material complete for the same.

R. SALE
Commanding Field Force

Captain J. Paton, Assistant Quarter-Master General, to Major-General Sir R. Sale

Cabool, November 9, 1841

I have the honour, by direction of Major-General Elphinstone, commanding in Afghanistan, to acquaint you that the condition of the force here is at present unfortunately such as to compel him to request you will march the troops under your command to its assistance immediately on receipt of this, at all risks and with the utmost possible expedition.

J. PATON

Major-General Sir R. Sale to Captain Paton

Jellalabad, November 15, 1841

I have to acknowledge the receipt of your letter of the 9th instant requiring the force under my command to move again upon Cabool. In reply I beg to represent that the whole of my camp equipage has been destroyed; that the wounded and sick have increased to upwards of 300; that there is no longer a single depot of provisions on the route; and that the carriage of the force is not sufficient to bring on one day's rations with it. I have at the same time positive information that the whole country is in arms and ready to oppose us in the defiles between this city and Cabool, whilst my ammunition is insufficient for more than two such contests, as I should assuredly have to sustain for six days at least.

With my present means I could not force the passes of either Jugduluk or Khoord Cabool, and even if the debris of my brigade did reach Cabool I am given to understand that I should find the troops now garrisoning it without the means of subsistence. Under these circumstances, a regard for the honour and interests of our government compels me to adhere to my plan, already formed, of putting this place into a state of defence, and holding it if possible, until the Cabool force falls back upon me or succours arrive from Peshawur or India.

Yesterday this city was invested by the enemy, amounting at the least to the lowest calculation to 5,000 men, which had kept up a heavy fire on the defective walls for upwards of 24 hours, by which we suffered much. I directed Lieutenant-Colonel Monteath, at the head of 700 bayonets, and the cavalry to sally forthwith and make a general attack. The enemy were totally routed at every point; but I must of course expect successive investments and to have to make unremitting efforts for our defence.

R. SALE

Sir W.H. Macnaghten to Captain Macgregor

Cabool, November 18, 1841

I have received your letters of the 13th instant. The cossid gave us an account of your action of the 14th instant, which, if he speaks truth, must have been a very successful one. We are in status quo. Our chief want is supplies. I perceive now that you could not well have joined us. I hope you have written to Mackeson, asking aid from the Sikhs under the treaty. If there is any difficulty about the Sikhs getting through the pass,

From Lady Sale's Diary

November 1, 1841
Our house is the best and most commodious. Sale had a shoke for gardening and had an excellent kitchen garden; whilst I cultivated flowers that were the admiration of the Afghan gentlemen who came to see us. My sweet peas and geraniums were much admired, but they were all eager to obtain the seed of the edible pea, which flourished well; and by being sown as soon as the frost was over we had plenty of succession crops, and we still have peas growing which we hope, if not cut off by frost, will give a crop next month.

The potatoes thrive well, and will be a very valuable addition to the cuisine. The cauliflowers, artichokes, and turnip radishes are very fine, and peculiarly mild in their flavour; they are all from seed we brought with us from our garden at Kurnaul. The Cabool lettuces are hairy and inferior to those cultivated by us; but the Cabool cabbages are superior, being milder, and the red cabbage from English seed grows well.

Regarding the fruits of Afghanistan, I should not be believed were I to state the truth. Selected grapes off a bunch of those in the Kohistan have been known to weigh 200 grains; the largest I ever weighed myself was 127 grains. It was the kind denominated the Bull's Eye by the English; I believe the natives call it the Hoosseinee-Angoor; its form is nearly round, and the taste very luscious; it is of a kind not generally purchasable. At Kardunah they grow in great perfection. Those I ate were sent as a present from a native gentleman to Captain Sturt, as were also some very delicious pears from Turkistan. The largest peaches I have myself weighed turned the scale at 15 rupees, and were fully equal in juiciness and flavour to those of the English hothouse. The finest are to be found in the Kohistan, but they are so delicate they will not bear carriage to Cabool. I have been assured by my friends who have been there in the peach season that the best fruit of the land at my table was quite inferior to those above mentioned. The Orleans blue plum is excellent. There is a green one resembling in appearance a greengage, but it is very tasteless. There are also many other kinds, with a great variety of melons, Water, Musk, and Surda, which is accounted the best.

November 2, 1841
This morning, early, all was in commotion in Cabool; the shops were plundered, and the people were all fighting.

Captain Sturt, my son-in-law, hearing that Captain Johnson's house and treasury (Captain Johnson is paymaster to the Shah's force) in the city were attacked, as also Sir Alexander Burnes's, went to General Elphinstone, who sent him with an important message, first to Brigadier Shelton at Siah Sung, and afterwards to the king (Shah Shuja) to concert with him measures for the defence of that fortress. Just as he entered the precincts of the palace, he was stabbed in three places by a well-dressed young man, who escaped into a building close by where he was protected by the gates being shut.

Fortunately for my son-in-law, Captain Lawrence had been sent to the king by the envoy, and sent Sturt home with a strong guard of 50 lancers, but they were obliged to make a long detour by Siah Sung. In the meantime, Lawrence came to tell me all that had passed, and to break the bad news to my daughter, Mrs Sturt.

I cannot describe how shocked I felt when I saw poor Sturt; for Lawrence, fearing to alarm us, had said he was only slightly wounded. He had been stabbed deeply in the shoulder and side, and on the face (the latter wound striking on the bone just missed the temple). He was covered with blood issuing from his mouth and was unable to articulate. From the wounds in the face and shoulder, the nerves were affected; the mouth would not open, the tongue was swollen and paralysed, and he was ghastly and faint from loss of blood. He could not lie down, from the blood choking him; and had to sit up in the palkee as best he might, without a pillow to lean against. With some difficulty and great pain he was supported upstairs, laid on his bed, and Dr Harcourt dressed his wounds, which having been inflicted about ten o'clock, now, at one were cold and stiff with clotted blood. The tongue was paralysed, and the nerves of the throat affected, so that he could neither swallow nor articulate; and the choking sensation of the blood in his throat was most painful to witness. He was better towards evening; and by his wife's unremitting attention in assisting him to get rid of the clotted blood from his mouth by incessant applications of warm wet cloths, he was by eleven at night able to utter a tolerably articulate sound. With what joy did we hear him faintly utter 'bet-ter'; and he really seemed to enjoy a teaspoonful of water, which we got into his mouth by a drop or two at a time, painful as it was to him to swallow it.

It was most gratifying to see the attention and kind feeling manifested on the occasion by the sergeants of the engineer department, and their anxiety (particularly Sergeant Deane's) to make themselves useful to Sturt.

Mackeson should offer a bribe to the Khybers, of a lac of rupees or more, to insure their safe passage. These are not times to stick at trifles.

The Goorkha regiment has been annihilated, but Pottinger and Haughton are here; the latter has lost his hand. I believe I told you that Paton lost his arm in the action we had near cantonments the other day. It is raining here, and the water is very cold, but I am not sure that this is not as bad for the enemy as for ourselves. I do not hear anything from Ghuznee or Candahar; but I should not wonder if they are in the same mess as ourselves; we must look for supplies chiefly from Peshawur.

Write to Mackeson continually; tell him to urge government to send as many troops into this country, and as speedily as possible. John Conolly is in the Bala Hissar with his majesty, who, as you may imagine, is in sad taking about all this fussad. I am making no progress in my negotiations with the rebels.

W.H. MACNAGHTEN

Major-General Sir R. Sale to Major Craigie

Jellalabad, November 24, 1841

The communication being on all sides interrupted, I am compelled to write in the most condensed form. Lest previous letters should have been intercepted, I would ask of you now to acquaint the commander-in-chief that the substance of our intelligence from Cabool is that a sudden and sanguinary insurrection broke out there on 2nd November. Armed bodies attacked simultaneously the houses of all the British residents in the city. Sir A. Burnes, his brother and Lieutenant Broadfoot were murdered. Brigadier Anquetil, Captains Johnson and Troup were fortunately at the moment in the cantonment. Captain Skinner has been secreted; Captain Mackenzie cut his way through the assailants (wounded).

The insurgents proceeded to establish themselves on the hills around the city; and, making an unexpected attack on our commissariat magazine, plundered it. There was a simultaneous rising in the Kohistan: the Shah's Goorkha battalion and his regiment of Kohistanees were both defeated and every officer put to the sword, excepting Major Pottinger and Lieutenant Haughton: the latter has lost one hand.

Our troops at Cabool maintained themselves on the two points of the Bala Hissar and the entrenched cantonment. They repelled several attacks on the latter and made a brilliant sally on the 5th. Actions were fought with varied success up to the 10th, on which day the British attacked, carried, with great slaughter, several forts and obtained very considerable supplies of provisions. The enemy assailed the cantonment on the 13th, but were repulsed with great loss, and two guns, which had been captured from the wuzeer, were retaken.

Since that time it would appear that there has been no engagement, but the investment continues, and the numbers of the enemy daily increase. All tribes are united against the Shah. The insurgents have proclaimed Mahomed Zeman Khan Barukzye, king; Jubbar Khan, wuzeer; and Abdoola Khan Atchakzye, the assassin of Sir A. Burnes, sirdar-i-sirdaran.

The earlier part of these events and transactions became known to me on the night of the 10th instant, at Gundamuck; and I was urged by General Elphinstone to advance to the succour of the capital, if I could place my sick and wounded in security. This was impossible; my ammunition also was insufficient for the operation; we had no supplies; and our carriage cattle were daily diminishing in number. I determined, therefore, to retire on Jellalabad. On the 11th the Jan-Bazees went over to the enemy, and they have since been followed by the Khyberee corps.

I reached this place on the 12th, after a successful rearguard affair, in which my cavalry charged and the enemy left 150 dead on the field. Five thousand men invested this place on the 13th; on the 14th I ordered a sally and general attack with part of my garrison. The enemy were totally routed, and I have since scarcely seen an armed Afghan around us, though a force is known to have assembled within a few miles. Incessant labour has put this place into a respectable state of defence. Eleven guns and five mortars are mounted on the works, which have now a widened rampart and growing parapet of three feet.

Meanwhile the Khyber is in a state of insurrection. Ali Musjid has been besieged; Captain Ferris's corps at Pesh Boluk was attacked, and it is believed that he only escaped with his people by concluding a convention with the assailants and retiring to Peshawur. We have, however, no certain information regarding him. I forward copy of General Elphinstone's last communication, written in French in consequence of its being known that the enemy have employed two young men, instructed in English in Delhi or Loodiana, to read our intercepted dispatches. I am happy to perceive that the general approves of my measures.

Captain Macgregor and I have written to Captain Mackeson to send up through the Khyber to us ammunition, treasure and provisions, and to call upon the Sikh government to aid us, according to treaty, with 5,000 troops. I can, in every event, I trust, maintain myself here for 30 days, and await reinforcement from India; and I should hope that Major-General Elphinstone will be enabled to retain possession of all he holds at Cabool. His excellency will not fail to perceive from the above detail that all measures of reinforcement and succour ought, at this crisis, to be prompt and energetic.

R. SALE

Copy of a letter from Major-General Elphinstone to the address of Sir R. Sale

Cabool, November 18, 1841

J'ai reçu votre lettre du 15 mo. Je pense que vous avez très bien fait si vous envoi des renforts de la place de Peshawur, et que vous vous trouvez dans la situation de nous aider, ne manquez pas de le faire; nous sommes dans un péril extrême.

Captain Lawrence, Assistant Agent to the Governor-General, Ferozepore, to Colonel Wild, Commanding at Ferozepore

November 14, 1841

I have the honour to request, with reference to the dispatch from Lieutenant Mackeson, which I showed you this morning, that the troops, now under orders for Cabool, should start with the least possible delay.

I would also suggest that the 60th Regiment, now in orders for Sukkur, and any other infantry regiment you may think proper, as well as the 10th Cavalry, should be held in immediate readiness for a move towards Afghanistan, as soon as instructions can arrive from Mr Clerk, agent governor-general, which will be the 19th instant, so that they could, without any difficulty, overtake the Kafila at the Ravee.

I would further offer my opinion that the commanding officer should not be hampered with any extra stores by the charge of ladies; but have under his care simply the treasure and such magazine stores as are deemed absolutely necessary for supplying the immediate wants of our troops in Afghanistan.

Perhaps you will agree with me that the better plan will be only to warn the officers of the corps above alluded to that they may be required to move, it being desirable to give as little room as possible for reports. In this view, I should not have suggested the ladies remaining behind, if their going now did not involve a certain degree of risk to themselves, and that they and their establishments must be in the way, should the troops be called on for any rapid movements.

H.M. LAWRENCE

PS Arrangements now in progress at the Ghaut will be completed by the 17th instant, and will enable me to cross the whole Kafila in one day.

Captain Mackeson to Mr Clerk

Peshawur, November 15, 1841

I have the honour to forward for your information a letter received this afternoon from Major-General Sale, commanding field force, dated Futteabad, 11th November. Several days before the receipt of this letter I had dispatched powder, etc. to Captain Macgregor sufficient for 100,000 rounds, but I am not positive that it has reached him, nor can I be that the quantity I shall now send will reach Jellalabad.

It appears that on General Sale's brigade leaving Gundamuck that post was again left to be guarded by Captain Burn's corps of Afreedees, Captain Dowson's Jan-Baz, and 200 of Captain Ferris's jezailchees. The whole of the Jan-Baz and one-third of Captain Burn's corps of Afreedees deserted and went over to the enemy, and the remainder refused to remain at Gundamuck. Captain Burn was consequently obliged also to retire with the remainder, and joined General Sale's column at Futteabad. He was unable to bring away with him from Gundamuck two of the Shah's guns, which had been left there for his protection, and it is not mentioned whether the guns were spiked on leaving them behind.

There can be no doubt that if the troops at Cabool do not succeed shortly in making the townspeople sue for terms, the tribes in Ningrahar, as well as those towards Cabool, will combine against us; and the force that moves from Ferozepore should consist of two brigades, with one, if not two regiments of Europeans. The brigades should follow each other as quickly as possible.

I have written to General Avitabile (in French, in order to avoid making use of a Persian writer) and for the information of Koonwur Purtab Sing, who is with Rajah Golab Sing and the Sikh troops in Hazara, an outline of the state of affairs at Cabool. I have told them that though I am in no alarm for the safety of our troops, either at Cabool or Jellalabad, still so long as they are confined to one spot the present rise among the Afghan race will extend every day; and as the Afghans about here have long ago declared that the Sikhs only hold Peshawur through the power of the British government, it became me, as a well-wisher to the two governments, to draw his attention to the small number of troops now at Peshawur and to recommend reinforcing them without delay.

I shall not think of asking for Sikh troops excepting in the last extremity, but the movement of a large force from Hazara to Peshawur, accompanied as they may perhaps be by the Koonwur himself, cannot fail to have a good effect.

F. MACKESON
Political agent

The Governor-General of India in Council to General Sir Jasper Nicolls

Fort William, December 3, 1841

We have received an express from Mr Clerk, of the 24th ultimo, containing information of the events at Cabool to the 9th, and at Jellalabad to the 15th ultimo.

These accounts exhibit a most unfavourable state of affairs at Cabool, but they do not lead us to alter the views and intentions which were stated in our yesterday's dispatch. Your Excellency will, therefore, expedite the movement of whatever may be required to complete one brigade, efficiently provided with all necessaries of equipment and supply, in the direction of Peshawur, to be stationed there, with orders of the tenor which [have been] fully explained, so as to give succour to our troops in the event of their retiring. We do not now desire to send a second brigade in advance, for we do not conceive it to be called for in view of the objects of support and assistance which we contemplate; and we think it inexpedient to detach any greater number of troops than may be absolutely indispensable from our own provinces.

It would be vain to speculate upon the issue of the contest at Cabool; but in the extreme event of the military possession of that city, and the surrounding territory, having been entirely lost, it is not our intention to direct new and extensive operations for the re-establishment of our supremacy throughout Afghanistan.

We can scarcely contemplate in such case that there will be any circumstances or political objects of sufficient weight to induce us to desire to retain possession of the remainder of that country, and, unless such shall be obvious as arising from the course of events, we should wish our military and political officers so to shape their proceedings as will best promote the end of retiring with the least possible discredit. Of course it will be desirable that this retirement shall be deliberate, and the result of arrangements that will leave some political influence in the country. But it is impossible to shut our eyes to the probability that the first impulse of the population in the southern districts, upon hearing of our having suffered disaster at Cabool, will be to rise and surround our different positions, cutting off the communication. In this case the commanding officers will be instructed to make it their first aim to fall back on the nearest support, and so to save their troops from the risk of being isolated; it being, of course, a paramount consideration to provide for the safety of the different detachments as far as possible. Major-General Nott, or the officer commanding at Candahar, will be directed, in the event of the loss of Cabool, to take the force at Ghuznee under his orders and to provide Colonel Palmer with suitable instructions. With regard to the regiment at Ghuznee, we shall instruct Mr Clerk to arrange with the Sikh government for giving every aid in its power, should the retirement of that corps to Dhera Ismael Khan, or other point on the frontier, be determined upon. We shall cause a copy of this paragraph to be conveyed to Major Rawlinson, Major-General Nott and Lieutenant-Colonel Palmer, both through Major Outram in Upper Sinde and Captain Mackeson in Peshawur.

We doubt not that your Excellency will have felt it desirable to superintend personally the execution of such measures on our frontier as the exigency of events may have rendered necessary and will, therefore, have proceeded to establish your headquarters at one of the advanced stations.

It is of high importance at this juncture that we should act in a clear and cordial plan of co-operation with the government of Lahore, and a dispatch has been this day in consequence addressed to Mr Clerk, of which we enclose a copy for your Excellency's information.

AUCKLAND
W.W. BIRD
W. CASEMENT
H.T. PRINSEP

Mr Maddock to Sir W.H. Macnaghten, Envoy and Minister at the Court of Shah Shuja-al-Mulk

Fort William, December 5, 1841

The latest accounts which have reached government from Cabool give information of the state of affairs at that place up to the 9th ultimo, and notwithstanding the difficulties with which the British forces were then surrounded, the governor-general in council entertains sanguine hopes that, aided by the zeal and gallantry of the troops, you will have been enabled to suppress the insurrection, or, at all events, to have secured a supply of provisions for the army, whereby it may be secure in its positions for the winter.

So serious appear to be the difficulties which are to be encountered at Cabool, amid a hostile population, by a force cut off for several months from support by the impassable state of the roads in the winter season, that the governor-general in council has felt compelled to take into his contemplation the possible occurrence of still more serious disaster to our troops there, and to provide even for the contingency of our political influence in that quarter being for a time entirely subverted; and the first duty of government in issuing instructions suitable to such an event having been discharged, I am now directed to assure you that the governor-general in council will remain anxiously mindful of your position, and that every measure will be adopted, as the tenor of the information received may show to be necessary, of which the season will admit, and which may be otherwise practicable, for affording relief to yourself and to the troops by whom you are accompanied.

A strong and complete brigade has been ordered from India and is now in progress to Peshawur, where it will be directed to act immediately in aid of Sir Robert Sale, who was by the last accounts posted at Jellalabad; and in the event of further operations being necessary in that quarter, his lordship in council has it in contemplation to relieve the 13th Light Infantry and 35th Native Infantry by two fresh regiments; and the movements of these or other corps which may be dispatched towards Peshawur will depend upon the events which may have occurred at Cabool, and upon the directions which you and General Elphinstone may think proper to issue.

Copies of the instructions which have been issued by the governor-general in council to his excellency the commander-in-chief will be communicated confidentially, through Mr Clerk, to Captain Mackeson, and you will be informed of their purport through him as opportunity may require and admit; but in every event you may depend on the desire and determination of the governor-general in council to afford all possible succour to your position, and you will have complete and timely information of the political views of his lordship in council, under any change of circumstances which may arise.

Major-General Nott will, of course, have been anxious to give you every assistance in his power from the troops at Candahar, and it would be a source of much satisfaction to the government to know that he has felt himself able to detach with a reasonable prospect of safety, at a season in which, ordinarily, many difficulties may be expected, any effective portion of those troops towards Cabool.

The remarks or directions of government must now be limited to the points which have here been noticed. We have only for the present to trust to an overruling

Providence, and to the energy and perseverance of our gallant troops, for the maintenance of the power and safety of our arms.

T.H. MADDOCK
Secretary to the government of India

The Governor-General of India in Council to General Sir Jasper Nicolls

Fort William, December 15, 1841

Upon reconsidering the latest intelligence which we have received, extending (though comprising no detailed particulars of facts) to the 18th November from Cabool and to the 23rd November from Jellalabad, and on a review of the large extent of available means which will be very shortly collected for the support of tranquillity within our own provinces, it has appeared to us likely that, on the discretion which we requested your Excellency to exercise in our dispatch of the 5th instant, you will have determined to send on Her Majesty's 9th Foot and a fifth native regiment to Peshawur, and to place Major-General Lumley in command of the force assembled on that frontier. We beg to intimate to your Excellency, that if you should have come to that decision, it is one of which we would cordially approve.

The objects of the force collected towards Peshawur would, as before stated to your Excellency, be mainly those of demonstration and strength upon that part of the Afghan frontier; but for these objects it may, as it seems to us on our present information, be advisable to employ two effective brigades under an officer of the high reputation and ability possessed by Major-General Lumley.

Should your Excellency have resolved to give effect to this arrangement, we would commit to Major-General Lumley the political as well as military direction of proceedings within the tracts wherein he will have to act. The political agents, Captain Macgregor and Captain Mackeson, will place themselves in subordination to him and will be guided by his orders.

Your Excellency will cause a copy of this intimation to be sent to those officers by Mr Clerk, if Major-General Lumley should proceed on this duty.

We shall hereafter communicate any detailed instructions which it may seem desirable to send, to Major-General Lumley, if so employed, but he will, in the first instance, be guided by the spirit of the dispatches addressed to your Excellency [earlier this month]. The safety of the troops under Sir Robert Sale will, of course, be the nearest and most prominent object of his care, and he will hold himself in such force towards the Ghilzie or other passes leading in advance of Jellalabad to Cabool (which will be closed for the winter) as circumstances will admit.

If there should be no longer a question of giving a support to the position of our troops at Cabool, and the supply of a force in, or in advance of, the Jellalabad valley should be difficult and precarious, it will be for Major-General Lumley to decide whether it will be expedient to remain in that forward position, in dependence on the receipt of provisions and material from the Peshawur territory, to the roads communicating with it in his rear. We should regard this as a matter to be regulated entirely by his military discretion, and on his knowledge of the present political ends which are contemplated by the government.

AUCKLAND
W.W. BIRD
WM CASEMENT
H.T. PRINSEP

Major-General Sir R. Sale to Major Craigie

Jellalabad, December 1, 1841

I have to request that you will acquaint the commander-in-chief that the enemy continue to occupy a position amongst hills, at the distance of about three miles from this place. I have reason to believe that their present numbers do not exceed 2,000, and they have not ventured on any serious movement since the 14th ultimo. Daily, however, they push forward parties in advance, which direct a desultory fire of musquetry upon the bastions and curtains to the north-westward.

From Cabool our direct latest intelligence is the letter of the 18th ultimo from Major-General Elphinstone. A spy, however, who visited the enemy's camp, reports to us that they there describe the situation of the Feringhees at the capital as similar to our own in Jellalabad, meaning that they are invested, subject to petty attacks, and anxiously awaiting reinforcements and supplies. We shall, indeed, be well pleased to hear that their position is not more unfavourable than our own.

Captain Mackeson writes us that he has continued to throw provisions into Ali Musjid and expects to be able to add a reinforcement of Eusofzyes. He also informs us that one regiment of native infantry was to leave Ferozepore on the 19th ultimo, another on the 20th and a third to march from Loodiana on the 21st.

We trust, if provisions can be obtained, that both the force at Cabool, and we at

Jellalabad, may be enabled, by God's blessing, to maintain ourselves until the arrival of these troops, should they be here early in January, but I must beg of you to make known explicitly to his excellency my opinion that the crisis in Afghanistan demands much larger reinforcements than this, and that European infantry and dragoons ought to form a part of it. I consider also the present artillery, in the eastern part of the country, viz., two batteries, to be insufficient; I would recommend that a third be added without delay, which ought to consist of 9-pounders.

I would also remind you that the whole of the camp equipage of the force now under my command, with the exception of the hospital tents, and one single sepoy pall of the 35th Regiment, has been destroyed, having been left in charge of the irregulars at Gundamuck, whose defection has been already reported. If also it be the intention of government to subjugate the provinces now in a state of universal revolt, it is to be remarked that there are, in this immediate vicinity, besides the strong place of Lughman, other forts which cannot be breached without the aid of siege artillery, or reduced without a complete engineer establishment guided by the most skilful officers.

R. SALE

Major-General Sir R. Sale to Major Craigie

Jellalabad, December 2, 1841

I have to request the favour of your informing the commander-in-chief that the enemy who had for some days annoyed my garrison, by sending forward parties to open a desultory fire on our soldiers labouring on the works, appeared in force yesterday morning, closely environed the northern and western faces and partially surrounded the whole place.

A desire, under present circumstances, to reserve our ammunition would, perhaps, have induced me to tolerate this audacity somewhat longer; but as these continued attacks had at length the effect of compelling our people to suspend their exertions to complete the parapets, and as the reports of our spies indicated an intention on the part of the rebels to establish mines under the scarp of our defences (a species of operation in which some Khails of this country are exceedingly skilful), I determined to remove them by a sally to a more convenient distance.

I therefore formed a column within the Cabool gate, consisting of 300 of the 13th, 300 of the 35th a detachment of sappers and jezailchees, two guns of No. 6 Light Field Battery and the whole of the cavalry. I placed this force under the immediate command of Lieutenant-

Colonel Dennie, purposing to superintend the operation myself from the ramparts.

On the gate being thrown open, the column advanced at a rapid pace, and then, according to my previous instructions, the sappers diverging to the left swept the whole space in front of the walls in that direction and moved towards the rocky mounds on the right of the main road from Cabool. The security of the other flank was in like manner provided for, by a company of the 35th being extended facing towards the river; whilst the cavalry had been ordered to follow the track of the main column and then, forming and wheeling to their left, to intercept all fugitives on the plain in that quarter. These movements were made in uninterrupted succession and with great spirit, and an animating cheer burst from our soldiers the moment they found themselves beyond the walls.

The enemy poured their fire upon Colonel Dennie's column as soon as it debouched, but, dismayed by the unchecked speed of its advance, they broke and, deserting the ruined forts in their rear, fled across the plain obliquely towards the river. They were promptly and hotly pursued up to its bank by the jezailchees and the skirmishers of the 13th; and Captain Abbott, pushing his guns at the gallop up to a point which commanded the stream, formed battery and completed the deroute. His practice here was excellent, and the enemy suffered visibly and severely from his round shot and shrapnel. Many of them fell under his fire and that of the infantry and irregulars, and many, rushing into the river and missing the ford in their consternation, got into deep water and were swept away and drowned.

The cavalry also successfully sought an opportunity of charging on the level and once more found ample employment for their sabres. The sappers, too, surprised by a sudden onset – a mass of the Ooloos moving on apparently with the intention of operating against the southern front of the walls – dispersed them with slaughter. The enemy now were in panic flight on every side, and, the reserves having been steadily reformed, the work of demolishing the walls of old forts that had afforded cover to petty assailants was commenced.

The effect of this sudden and unexpected blow has been electrical. The insurgents have not only fled from the near holds of the Zilne Urbol and two others, in which the Ghilzie chiefs Aziz Khan and Gool Mahomed, and Golain Jon, son of the revolted Urz Bezie, had taken up their quarters, but retired from the whole line of the Char Bhag forts, and only rallied at Ummar Khail, at the cautious distance of 12 miles from our ramparts. The latest information is to the effect that the rebel commander has demanded a strong reinforcement of horse from Cabool as an indispensable condition of his making any further attempts against us. Our loss has been trifling beyond calculation or hope.

R. SALE

Captain Mackeson to Mr Clerk

Futteghur, December 2, 1841

On receipt of copy of Sir W.H. Macnaghten's letter to the address of Captain Macgregor, dated Cabool, 18th November 1841, in which I am desired to ask for 'aid from the Sikhs under the treaty' and 'to urge government to send as many troops into this country, and as speedily as possible', I lost no time in again calling on General Avitabile to send five or six thousand men to Jellalabad.

General Avitabile consulted with the commanding officers of the four Mussulman auxiliary battalions now at Peshawur. These officers made objections to ordering their men to march. The principal were: *First*, that the four battalions could not parade more than 2,200 fighting men fit for service; that this small body could not make its way to Jellalabad; and that on reaching Lalpura it would be surrounded by overpowering numbers of the Ooloos. *Second*, that there were no troops at Peshawur, either for the protection of Peshawur in their absence, or to march to their support, and that their supplies would be cut off. *Third*, that when they last marched with our troops towards Cabool, after passing Khyber, their own government took no measures to provide for them, although Koonwur Kharall Sing and Nao Nehal Sing were then at Peshawur with 40,000 men; and that when they applied to Colonel Wade to be supplied from the company's godowns, they were told that they must look to their own government to provide for them. What hope, therefore, could they now have that they would be supported, when there were no troops at Peshawur? *Fourth*, one of the Nujib battalions had been completely annihilated in the Khyber Pass, and no measures taken, either by the Sikh or the British government, to save them. *Finally*, that the promises of extra pay made to them had never been fulfilled, and that although the semblance of discipline was still kept up in the Sikh army, it was well known that the sepoys no longer obeyed or had any fear of their officers; and they feared that these battalions, if ordered to march to Jellalabad, would break out into open mutiny, an event which might encourage the Afghan tribes round Peshawur to imitate the example of the tribes at Cabool.

I had offered General Avitabile to pay the troops a gratuity of two months' pay, or 20,000 rupees, if they would march towards Jellalabad 4,000 strong, and this had been made known to the commandants.

I have no fresh intelligence from Cabool. Mulla Najaib, the pensioner of the British government, returned to Peshawur from Cabool a few days ago. He was in Cabool up to the action of the 14th, and there had been no action since; but friends of his, who had left Cabool eight days later than he had, told him that the Caboolees were meditating another attack on the cantonment troops and were waiting the arrival of those

Kohistanees who had hitherto been held in check and occupied with the Goorkha corps. Mulla Najaib states that there had been four great actions, in all of which our troops had been successful, and he expressed great admiration of our mode of fighting. He compared the sallies of our troops with their artillery to the thunder-flash, rapid and carrying destruction wherever it alighted.

I desired Mulla Najaib to draw out an account of what he had seen and heard, which I will send you on some future occasion. I learn from him that, on the first outbreak, the Shah sent his own battalion, under Mr Campbell and Nizamood Dowlah, to seize the rebels in the city; but after a great struggle, and much loss, they failed. His majesty also entreated our troops, who had been marched to the Bala Hissar, to go in support of his own; but they pleaded that their orders were to remain in the Bala Hissar and near his person.

Captain Skinner was seized by the rebels in the shop of a seller of wood, where he had been concealed some days. He is now made to read any letters of ours that fall into their hands; there is also a son of Cazi Mulla Hussan, educated at Loodiana, who is in the city of Cabool, who reads these letters.

A detachment of 300 men coming up to Cabool from Ghuznee is said to have been annihilated by the Warduk tribe. Another detachment of Afghan Dooranee Horse of similar strength to the above, bringing up the Zamin Dawar prisoners from Candahar towards Cabool, had been overpowered on the other side of Ghuznee in an engagement with the tribes. A European officer commanded; but he reached Ghuznee with a few horsemen in safety. The troops at Ghuznee are said to have put to death two of the principal Afghans in the city there. No disaster is mentioned by Mulla Najaib as having occurred to the garrison there, and there is reason to hope that our troops will weather the storm much better at Candahar than at Cabool.

F. MACKESON
Political agent

Major Craigie to Brigadier F. Wild

Camp, Secundra, December 11, 1841

I have the honour, by direction of the commander-in-chief, to inform you that the governor-general in council has been pleased to confer on you the rank of a brigadier of the second class whilst in command of the troops proceeding to the Afghan frontier. You will, therefore, take the advanced portion of that force, consisting of the 60th and

64th regiments, under your orders.

As you may not have any statement of the troops, supplies and stores proceeding under Lieutenant-Colonel Tulloch's protection, I am desired to insert the information:

Sikh Motimud commandant, Ghyare Sing	
British commandant, Mohamed Hoosain	
60th Regiment Native Infantry	900
Fighting 64th Native Infantry	1,048
3rd Local Horse	100
Sappers	137
Golundauze	164
Syces and followers	855
Horses	247
Camel loads of ordnance stores	166
Commissariat camels	137
Baggage, etc., camels	540
Camel loads of 8 lacs of treasure	100
Officers	36

You are well aware that Her Majesty's 9th Foot and the 26th Native Infantry are preparing to cross the Punjab; but as you may be called upon to act before the arrival of Major-General McCaskill, I am desired by his excellency to convey to you the following instructions, prepared under the orders of the governor-general in council.

Your brigade will be concentrated at or near Peshawur, to establish a point of union and support in case of emergency. It will assist in putting down, if not completely, by its presence, controlling and checking any disposition which the insurgents of Khyber and the vicinity may evince to extend their depredations to the eastward of the pass. You will consider yourself authorized to aid the force of our ally, the ruler of the Punjab; in such case, retaining in your own hands, however, the command of any portion of your troops so employed; and not diverging much from the line between Peshawur and Ali Musjid.

The situation of Major-General Sir Robert Sale will be fully made known to you by Captain Mackeson; it is not so bad as was at first supposed, but still it has not a certain supply of provisions; money is scarce; and the stock of ammunition decreases.

If you feel confident of your ability to advance with three corps to Jellalabad, and to maintain the integrity of your communication with Peshawur (aided by the 4th), you are authorized to make that forward movement. You are to be guided by your own judgement in this; the commander-in-chief being so favourably impressed with an opinion that you merit a high degree of confidence that he does not invest Major-General Sir Robert Sale with any power to order you onwards.

Obtain the fullest intelligence from Captain Mackeson; weigh the advantages and difficulties; study the nature of the enemy and of the pass; ascertain the number and positions of your opponents; and then decide for yourself.

You have not at present any guns; but you have artillerymen, sappers and miners, and officers of both corps. His excellency is not aware of any difficulty likely to prevent your being accommodated by the Sikh governor, General Avitabile, with four or six pieces, and you will solicit such aid, when necessary, through Captain Mackeson.

As your object will be to restore our communications and to replenish the magazine, treasury and commissariat at Jellalabad, you should be as lightly equipped yourselves as climate will allow; but escort as large a convoy as you safely can. Ammunition first; then money; finally, supplies of food, preferring the least bulky.

It is too early yet to furnish you with any ulterior instructions; of course, when arrived at Jellalabad, you fall under the command of Major-General Sir Robert Sale, to whom the necessary communications will be made.

Should collision arise between the Sikh forces in the Peshawur territory and the Afghan inhabitants of that country, you will attend to the wishes of the political agent on that subject. If further misfortune should attend our troops at Cabool and Jellalabad, you are not to consider such events as being sufficient reasons for remaining fixed at or near Peshawur; on the contrary, you should then resolutely attack and firmly occupy several points in the Khyber Pass, to secure their retreat with credit. This, however, is only mentioned as a contingency.

Keep up a correspondence with Sir Robert Sale, for which, it is hoped, Captain Macgregor and Captain Mackeson will always be able to find means. Small detachments, or weak posts, are to be avoided. Captain Mackeson is aware of two passes by which the Khyber can be turned; the commander-in-chief would have you be cautious in having two lines of operation, unless they are so near that the firing may be mutually heard and paths of communication be available. The adoption of either of these new lines must be a subject on which to exercise your judgement.

Mr Clerk prepared last year a paper of hints to officers passing through the Punjab; no doubt you have been furnished with a copy.

In conclusion, his excellency directs me to ask for an acknowledgement of this dispatch, and for a report of your proceedings, at least every second day, whilst you are acting independently. Concerning Sikh affairs and Sikh troops, you will communicate freely with Mr Clerk and Captain Mackeson.

P. CRAIGIE

Major-General Sir Robert Sale to Major Craigie

Jellalabad, December 10, 1841

The enemy have not ventured on even a demonstration towards Jellalabad since the 1st instant. The hostile chiefs are still at Ummar Khail, 12 miles distant, but are said to have few followers and to be distracted with dissensions among themselves and between them and the rebel leaders at Cabool. We have received some further account of the affair of the 23rd ultimo in the environs of that capital. Our ultimate success on that day does not seem doubtful, but our troops met with a check in the first onset, and a gun fell into the hands of the enemy.

Lieutenant-Colonel Oliver, 5th Native Infantry, Captain Mackintosh, of the same corps, and Lieutenant Lang, 27th, were killed; and Captain Walker, Irregular Horse, died of his wounds. On the part of the insurgents Meer Musjide, the most influential chief of the Kohistanees, fell; and Abdoola Khan Atchakzye, the assassin of Sir A. Burnes, was wounded.

R. SALE

General Sir Jasper Nicolls to the Governor-General of India in Council

Delhi, December 24, 1841

I have the honour to acknowledge the receipt, this morning, of your Lordship's dispatch of the 15th instant by express.

My receipt last night of an express from Mr Clerk, dated 21st instant, with 13 enclosures, all of which have been of course communicated by him to government, removed all remaining doubt as to the propriety of directing Her Majesty's 9th Foot and the 26th Native Infantry to follow the brigade under Brigadier Wild, which they will accordingly do early next month.

The repeated calls for cavalry, and your Lordship's opinion given in the second paragraph of your dispatch of the 2nd instant, have induced me to order the 10th Cavalry to march with Major-General McCaskill – which will, I hope, be approved under the circumstances stated by Mr Clerk and quoted in my dispatch to your Lordship in Council on the 20th instant. In addition to the two 9-pounder guns and 24-pounder howitzer, ordered to move with the Major-General, I beg to apprise your Lordship that five other pieces, indented for by Captain Abbott, will accompany this convoy.

In obedience to your Lordship's wishes that Major-General Lumley should be placed in command of the force assembling at Peshawur, I requested his attendance at my tent and placed the dispatch, now acknowledged, in his hands. The general is willing to proceed, but requested that his medical adviser should be consulted as to his ability to undertake such a service. Assistant Surgeon Tunner decidedly assured me that his state of health would by no means admit of the required exertion and exposure. In this dilemma, I have ordered Major-General Pollock to proceed to Ferozepore and there assume the charge, that is, the military command.

J. NICOLLS

Mr Maddock to General Sir Jasper Nicolls

Fort William, January 3, 1842

We have received your Excellency's dispatch of the 24th ultimo and deeply as we regret that the state of Major-General Lumley's health should have deprived the government of his services in the important post which we had proposed that he should hold, we are satisfied with the judiciousness of the selection which your Excellency has made for his successor in the person of Major-General Pollock. That officer will be vested with the same political authority beyond the Indus which we had designed to confer on Major-General Lumley, and he should be instructed to place himself in direct and confidential communication with Mr Clerk, as the chief political authority charged with the control of British interests on our north-west frontier, and in the territories of Lahore.

Captain Mackeson and the other subordinate political authorities in the eastern provinces of Afghanistan will be apprised of the major-general's appointment to these duties and directed to seek their instructions from him for the date of his crossing the Indus, and to keep him fully informed of the state of affairs in that quarter during his march across the Punjab.

We have resolved to appoint Lieutenant Sir Richmond Shakespeare to hold the office of secretary to Major-General Pollock, and we trust that the talents of this officer, by which his late services in Central Asia have been distinguished, will prove of much advantage to the major-general in the field of operations now open to him.

AUCKLAND
W.W. BIRD
WM CASEMENT
H.T. PRINSEP

Major Craigie to Brigadier Wild

Delhi, December 26, 1841

On the 11th instant I had the honour to convey to you in a dispatch, No. 2360, the general instructions of the commander-in-chief for your guidance in the important command to which you have been nominated, and I am now required to express the apprehension of his excellency that the communication may have miscarried or been delayed in transit, otherwise the receipt of so interesting a paper would at once have been acknowledged; a duplicate of the dispatch has accordingly been prepared, and will be transmitted with the present letter.

I have been instructed to take the present opportunity to apprise you that Her Majesty's 9th Foot and the 26th Native Infantry, with the 10th Regiment of Light Cavalry and half of No. 5 Light Field Battery, have been ordered to march towards Peshawur without any unnecessary delay.

Major-General Pollock, CB, has been selected for the chief command of the forces, and Captain Ponsonby, now at Peshawur, will be attached to the major-general as his assistant adjutant-general. You will therefore require that officer to await at Peshawur the arrival of Major-General Pollock.

The infantry of the force will be divided into two brigades. The first brigade, consisting of Her Majesty's 9th Foot and 26th and 53rd regiments of native infantry, will be commanded by Major-General McCaskill. The second brigade will be composed of the 30th, 60th and 64th regiments and will be under your orders, with Captain Lottie as your brigade-major. This distribution of the troops into brigades is not, however, to interfere with your command of the four battalions, and you will consider the instructions you have received as fully applicable to the present state of affairs as when they were first prepared. The commander-in-chief has again carefully considered these instructions, and he does not observe that he can improve them.

If you are confident that you can pass through the Khyber Pass with your four corps, it is, his excellency observes, certainly of importance to show the Afghan nation how speedily (distance considered) we can repair our misfortunes; but you are not unnecessarily to run any very great risk. You will let the convoy for Jellalabad be as large as considerations of security will warrant, bearing in mind that ammunition is a primary consideration, then treasure and then food.

Ali Musjid ought to be occupied with three companies of native infantry, well provisioned, and with a good store of ammunition; its defences must also be repaired. The remainder of the corps furnishing the garrison should be posted further in the pass, in some defensible and commanding position; at this season it is hoped that no unhealthiness prevails to prevent this arrangement. With the four corps of infantry, Captain Ferris's corps of jezailchees should advance.

If either of the northern passes is attempted, the commander-in-chief desires that the operation may be undertaken by the Sikh troops, keeping the Khyber to our own native infantry, and by no means mixing the two forces. With two established posts in the Khyber, the commander-in-chief anticipates no serious difficulty in the advance of the infantry and cavalry under Major-General Pollock.

P. CRAIGIE

Major-General Sir Robert Sale to Major Craigie

Jellalabad, December 13, 1841

Being doubtful whether the previous cossids have reached Peshawur, and a dawk having been now established along the margin of the Cabool River, by which three small packets have come safely to this place, I think it advisable to recapitulate, for his excellency's information, part of the contents of mine of the 10th instant.

Since their defeat on the 1st, the enemy have not ventured on even a demonstration towards Jellalabad. We have received some further accounts of the affair in the environs of Cabool, on the 23rd ultimo. It does not appear doubtful that the ultimate success of the British on that day was decisive; but the troops experienced a check at the first onset, and a gun was captured by the enemy; the loss was heavy on both sides.

On ours, Lieutenant-Colonel Oliver, Captain Mackintosh, 5th Regiment Native Infantry and Lieutenant Laing, 27th, were killed; and Captain Walker, 4th Regiment Irregular Cavalry, has died of his wounds. On the part of the insurgents, Meer Musjide, the most influential chief in the Kohistan, Abdoola Khan Atchakzye, the assassin of Sir A. Burnes, and many other men of note and distinction have fallen. Our spies report that another action was fought at the village of Wazirabad, near Cabool, on the 4th instant, which terminated most favourably to us; but no communication has reached us on this subject from the Bala Hissar or the cantonment.

As regards the situation and prospects of the troops at Jellalabad, I must again ask of you to remind his excellency that the whole of our camp equipage was destroyed at Gundamuck, and it must be supplied again to enable us to take the field. Our soldiers are on half rations, and we have provisions at the full rate for six weeks. The troops are healthy, as the accompanying state will show, although they labour six hours daily on the fortifications, and there are not three full reliefs for the guards on the walls.

Treasure is urgently required, officers and men being from two to three months in arrears; and our commissariat's arrangements are cramped for want of the means of disbursements. I have mentioned that I have no official details of the affairs at Cabool; but from all that I can glean of their nature I conclude that the expenditure of ordnance ammunition has been very great, and that a large supply, especially of grape and shrapnel, ought to accompany the reinforcements.

Captain Mackeson informs us, under date of the 10th instant, that a ressalah, in charge of ammunition, was to cross the Attock on that day; and that the first brigade of infantry has passed the Jhelum. Whilst on the subject of reinforcement, I would beg to reiterate my recommendation that a siege train of heavy ordnance be sent here, without which many of the forts of the refractory chiefs cannot be reduced; also that engineer officers capable of conducting the attack of a place accompany it. At present there is one only at Cabool, and he is permanently attached to Shah Shuja.

The regiments of infantry of my brigade urgently require clothing if not relieved this season. I am given to understand that a part of that of the 13th was lost some time since, in boats on the Ganges, and the 35th has now in wear its coats of 1838. Both need watchcoats.

R. SALE

General Sir J. Nicolls to the Governor-General in Council

Camp, one march north of Delhi, December 28, 1841

The accompanying dispatch, dated 13th instant, from Major-General Sir Robert Sale has already been submitted to your Lordship in Council through the military department; but as Sir Robert has repeated his suggestion that 'a siege train of heavy ordnance be sent forward', without which 'many of the forts of the refractory chiefs cannot be reduced', I think it necessary to bring this subject to your Lordship's notice.

Before we could send this train by Jellalabad, and collect, with extreme difficulty and some risk, the troops which should accompany it, we shall know how Sir William Macnaghten and General Elphinstone have been able to repel or disperse the insurgents. If an amnesty should be granted, we cannot require this great armament. If the rebels are obliged to relinquish their undertaking and to return home in despair, are we to arouse them again by following them into their valleys and fastnesses?

It may be most just and expedient to punish two or three of the greatest traitors by levelling their strongholds; but war against tribes seems so closely to resemble a resolution to subdue the country again, at whatever cost, that I cannot sanction even preparation for such an object, without your Lordship in Council's express orders.

Intimately connected with these repeated suggestions that a heavy train should be sent on are the recommendations of Captain Macgregor and Captain Mackeson (equally frequent and more urgent) that 10,000 or 12,000 troops, including three or more European regiments, should be sent via the Punjab into Afghanistan.

When the corps march next week, the numbers already moving on Peshawur will exceed 7,000 men; and beyond this great reinforcement, I shall most unwillingly spare a man from the Sirhind or Meerut Divisions, except for the February convoy.

In reply to Mr Secretary Maddock's dispatch of 18th instant, I have the honour to state that the 3rd Native Infantry has been ordered to proceed to Saugor, in order to enable the general officer commanding there to relieve the Madras troops at Jubbulpore and Husinjabad. A regiment will be sent from Benares to Mirzapur to enable the 3rd to move without any avoidable delay.

J. NICOLLS

H.T. PRINSEP

Resolution by the Government of India

Fort William, January 6, 1842

In the conduct of military operations at the present crisis in Afghanistan and the adjoining countries, it appears to the governor-general in council to be of all things most essential to attend to the expedience, the safety and the necessity of military movements with reference to military considerations in the first place. These will doubtless always be affected more or less by political circumstances, but they should be under the control of such circumstances no further than commanding officers – responsible for their own military arrangements and for the honour and success of the troops committed to their charge – may see fitting.

T.H. MADDOCK

The Governor-General of India in Council to the Secret Committee

Fort William, January 22, No. 9, 1842

With reference to our dispatch in this department, under date the 9th instant, per India steamer, submitting a précis of our latest information regarding the state of affairs in

Afghanistan, we have now to communicate, with the deepest regret, the melancholy intelligence, such as it has yet reached us, of the treacherous murder of the envoy and minister, Sir William Macnaghten, at a conference to which he was invited in furtherance of negotiations for the withdrawal of our troops.

We pass over the reports of a somewhat improved state of affairs at Cabool, which had reached us at different dates, previously to the receipt of this intelligence. From our dispatch of the 9th instant, your Honourable Committee will be aware of the unsatisfactory accounts which had reached us from Cabool to 9th December. From that date to the 25th, we have no letter from any of the British officers, either of the Cabool mission or force; but it appears certain that about 13th or 15th December Sir William Macnaghten judged it necessary to make overtures to the Afghan chiefs in arms against us, on the basis of our evacuation of the positions which we held at the capital.

While these overtures were under discussion, supplies were obtained in the cantonment, which gave rise to the more favourable reports that your Honourable Committee will find in letters of different dates, from Jellalabad and Peshawur. Mahomed Akbar Khan, son of Dost Muhammad Khan, who had escaped from confinement at Bokhara, and was proceeding to Cabool to deliver himself up to the envoy and minister, found the insurrection in full violence on his arrival and immediately took a prominent part in it. He appears to have been the channel through which Sir William Macnaghten's negotiations for withdrawal were carried on, and was believed in the country to be disposed in some measure to aid our interests.

What the motives were which induced him to take the life of Sir William Macnaghten, by an act which seems to have been one of the most gross and barbarous perfidy, we do not yet know with accuracy, but the fact of the murder is placed beyond doubt by the brief note of Major Pottinger of December 25th, and by the concurrent tenor of all the reports which have reached Jellalabad. The letter from Cabool of the son of the governor of Jellalabad to his father of the latter place, of which your Honourable Committee will find a translation appended to Mr Clerk's dispatch of the 12th instant, gives all the detail of which we are in possession up to this time respecting this deplorable event.

We await further and more accurate reports before we decide on the measures which it may be becoming to pursue in consequence of this bloody outrage, and we must also very anxiously await these reports so that we may learn the fate of the troops which appear to have been reduced to a state of most imminent peril at Cabool. We need not assure your Honourable Committee that, on the first occasion of which circumstances will admit, we will cause the strictest inquiry to be made in regard to the military proceedings of which we are now compelled to anticipate that the result will be so calamitous.

It has been our first duty to determine whether further reinforcements ought to be forwarded to strengthen our position on the Afghan frontier, and your Honourable Committee will observe that we have immediately instructed his excellency the commander-in-chief to prepare another efficient brigade with cavalry and artillery for an advance to Peshawur, that we have authorized, under the sanction given by the honourable court, the raising of another regiment of regular cavalry, and that we have taken measures for adding to the efficiency of the force of artillery in the north-western provinces.

It may be satisfactory to your Honourable Committee to be informed that after the march of this further brigade, if it should be ordered to move beyond the Indus, we shall still have an army of 15,000 men (after providing for the security of all stations and cantonments) available for concentration and service on our north-western frontier.

We proceed to notice shortly such other papers connected with this subject as may appear to be of prominent interest.

Punjab and Peshawur

The correspondence here referred to regards the co-operation of the troops of the Lahore government. Captain Mackeson writes on the 25th ultimo that they still showed symptoms of insubordination.

In his letter Captain Mackeson strongly recommended the employment of a body of 700 Patan horsemen, who had last year accompanied our troops through the Khyber Pass. These men seemed willing to serve us, and their example, he observed, might have the effect of shaming the Sikh troops into a proper sense of their duty. He represented, however, that they complained of the non-fulfilment of some promise of extra pay which they alleged to have been made to them on the occasion of their former employment in the Khyber. Mr Clerk has, as will be seen, authorized Captain Mackeson to fulfil, insofar as the British and Afghan governments are concerned, any promise of extra pay that may have actually been made to the Sikh troops whilst serving beyond the Khyber last year.

We have approved of Mr Clerk's proceedings on this occasion and called on Sir C.M. Wade for an explanation of the grounds of the claim to extra batta which has been advanced by the Patans while employed in the Khyber.

Khyber

According to our latest information, this pass continued open. Captain Mackeson mentions having paid the Maliks of Khyber 4,000 rupees, on the condition of their dispersing their tribes from Ali Musjid and keeping the pass quiet, and he also mentions that the Afreedee Maliks had been holding jirga for several days, and that the result of their deliberations (previously, however, to the receipt of the latest tidings from Cabool) had been to keep the pass open, not to molest our convoys or dawks, and to punish the parties who had stopped the dawk some days previously.

In a letter dated 3rd instant Captain Mackeson mentions that Turebaz Khan, the friendly Mohmund chief, through whom our communications with Jellalabad had latterly been carried on, apprehended another attack from his rival Saadut Khan, and that he had assisted him with funds for the preservation of his position.

Jellalabad

Captain Macgregor writes to Captain Mackeson on the 27th ultimo that they were all continuing to do well at Jellalabad. He has acknowledged the receipt of 25,000 out of the 50,000 rupees sent to him by Captain Mackeson through the agency of Turebaz Khan, and he expected that the balance then at Lalpura would be sent on as soon as Turebaz Khan heard of the safe arrival of the first consignment.

Reinforcements

With advertence to our letter No. 2, we beg to transmit the accompanying copy of the commander-in-chief's further instructions to Brigadier Wild, authorizing him to entertain a body of jezailchees for service in the Khyber.

The documents here referred to regard the deputation of Captain Lawrence to act in conjunction with Brigadier Wild and Captain Mackeson in Peshawur, and the orders issued by the Lahore durbar to its officers in Peshawur, to co-operate with our troops. On 3rd January Captain Mackeson reported that the four corps of native infantry were then encamped within one march of Ali Musjid. He said they had four guns made over to us by the Sikh authorities in camp, and he was in hopes that 700 Patan horsemen in the service of the Sikhs would be ready to accompany them next day.

Orders, it appeared, continued to reach General Avitabile for the advance into Khyber of the Mussulman auxiliaries, in support of our troops; but it was supposed that they would not be able, owing to the want of pay, and the defectiveness of the arrangements for obtaining supplies, to advance beyond Ali Musjid. Mehtele Singh, with four Sikh battalions, was reported to have arrived at Attock, and Keishree Singh, with troops from Lahore, at Wazirabad, on his way to Peshawur.

Candahar

We have received no authentic intelligence from Candahar since the date of our last report of the 9th instant, per India steamer. Owing to the reports of a hostile feeling against us having arisen on the part of some of the tribes, between Candahar and Killa Abdoollah, it had been deemed prudent, by our authorities at Quetta, to withdraw our detachment from that post. This detachment accordingly reached Quetta on the 21st ultimo, with loss of only five stragglers and the private property of the officers, which had been voluntarily left behind for the purpose of saving ammunition and public stores.

Reports were current of an intended attack upon Quetta, but that place, with a reinforcement of 100 men of Her Majesty's 41st Foot and a wing of a regiment of native infantry was believed to be quite safe against any force the insurgents could bring against it. It was subsequently stated that the intention to attack Quetta had been for the time abandoned by the rebels, and that the leader of the force destined for that purpose had been recalled to Cabool. Major Outram appeared to place confidence in the fidelity of the Murrees and Kakurs to their late engagements, and thought that they had refused to listen to the seditious overtures of the traitor naib of Shawl.

Up to the date of our latest information, tranquillity prevailed in Sinde and Beloochistan, and though Major Outram appeared to omit no measure of precaution, he did not seem to apprehend any disturbance within the sphere of his jurisdiction; but your Honourable Committee will be in possession of later intelligence from this quarter, direct through Bombay, than any that we can furnish from hence.

Dost Muhammad Khan

On the receipt of authentic intelligence of Mahomed Akbar Khan's having assassinated Sir William Macnaghten, Mr Clerk directed Captain Nicolson to make Dost Muhammad a close prisoner, preventing all communication with him or his retinue by Afghans or Hindoostanees, except with his, Captain Nicolson's, permission. Further, giving him authority to increase the guard over the ex-Ameer's camp.

We have approved of Mr Clerk's proceedings, and intimated an opinion that similar precautions should be taken to ensure the safe custody of all members of the Ameer's family now in Hindoostan; but that no severity of treatment should be practised, beyond what may be required for such custody, and if the Ameer should particularly desire to have one or two members of his family brought from Loodiana to reside with him, the indulgence, under the precautions indispensable to prevent escape, may be granted to him.

AUCKLAND
W.W. BIRD
WM CASEMENT
H.T. PRINSEP

Major Craigie to Brigadier Wild

Camp, Burki-Chokie, December 30, 1841

I am directed by the commander-in-chief to request that you will consider whether, for the advance through the Khyber Pass, or for the subsequent security of it, it may be advantageous to employ a body of jezailchees, of the Eusofzye or other tribe, which may be depended upon.

If so, you are authorized to entertain a body of 300 of those men for these services, consulting Captain Mackeson as to the conditions of service, suitable method of treatment and rates of pay. It is considered by government that the weapon wielded by the Afghan soldiery would be of great value, in aid of the ordinary arms of our troops, in all operations in mountain defiles.

If Captain Ferris has been entertaining men for his corps, and can afford such a detachment, or join you himself, it seems to his excellency desirable that either should be done. Should you, however, raise men independently of his corps, you must carefully select an officer or two to superintend and command them.

P. CRAIGIE

General Sir Jasper Nicolls to the Governor-General of India in Council

Paniput, January 1, 1842

I have the honour to acknowledge the receipt of the dispatch addressed to me by your Lordship in Council, and to express the great satisfaction which I have felt on receiving your Lordship's approval of the instructions issued to Brigadier Wild on the 11th December.

Respecting cavalry, I trust that the three ressalah attending the two first detachments will be sufficient for an early passage of the Khyber Pass. If delay be necessary, the 10th Cavalry will have joined.

I have the honour to enclose a copy of a letter addressed to Brigadier Wild, on the 30th ultimo, regarding the employment of a body of jezailchees, which I hope will meet with your Lordship's approbation.

I beg to report that, in conformity with the suggestion contained in your Lordship's dispatch, I have directed Her Majesty's 39th Regiment to march via Gwalior to Agra. Captain Taylor's levy has been ordered to remain at Cawnpore till further orders.

J. NICOLLS

The Governor-General of India in Council to General Sir Jasper Nicolls

Fort William, January 17, 1842

We entirely approve of the measures reported to have been adopted in your Excellency's letter of the 1st instant, and of the instructions issued to Brigadier Wild, authorizing him to entertain a body of jezailchees.

AUCKLAND
W.W. BIRD
WM CASEMENT
H.T. PRINSEP

Brigadier Wild to Major-General Sir R. Sale

Camp, Kowulsur, half-way to Jamrud, January 7, 1842

I had the honour to address a letter for your information to your brigade-major on the 27th ultimo, the day on which I reached Peshawur.

On the 1st instant I acknowledged the receipt of your letter of the 26th ultimo, and explained at the same time my reasons for not complying with your wish of proceeding to Jellalabad forthwith. Four guns have since been obtained from General Avitabile; but one of them, on being tested with an extra charge, smashed its limber, which is now in course of being replaced.

Another great difficulty under which we labour is the obstreperous conduct of our hired camel men, a large proportion of which seem not inclined to yield to the influence of either threats or money, and without supplies it is almost impossible to proceed, where man and beast depend on the food that accompanies the force for their subsistence.

In the third place, Captain Mackeson has offered terms to certain Afreedee chiefs for facilitating the passage through the Khyber Pass, to which the expected reply has not been received, and which so much affects the comparative security of our advance as to deserve serious attention, for there is no doubt that, if the brigade should meet the opposition of numerous bodies in many points during its progress, a heavy sacrifice of life must ensue, for the attempt once made must be persevered in to its fulfilment.

In the fourth instance, there is such an evident want of zealous co-operation on the part of the Sikh chiefs and soldiery, if not of their government – though I suspect the feeling originates there – that I consider no reliance can be placed on them for keeping open the communication in our rear after we have once gone on.

I have now the honour of acknowledging the receipt today of your note calling on me to hasten my advance, though at the same time it would appear that within the walls of Jellalabad you consider yourself safe, and it therefore remains for me to weigh maturely how far, with the inadequate means at my disposal, having no cavalry, except one troop of Irregular Horse, I would promote or hurt the interests of the service if, after pushing on, I were to join you in a crippled state. But if you thought of retiring with your force upon Peshawur, I would not hesitate instantly to advance and take up positions in the Khyber Pass, at any cost, to assist in facilitating your retreat.

I beg at the same time to assure you that I will not cease to watch for the first seasonable opportunity to advance with the force at my disposal, with a view to instantly avail myself of it.

C.F. WILD

Major Pottinger and Major-General Elphinstone to Captain Macgregor

Cabool, December 29, 1841

It having been found necessary to conclude an agreement, founded on that of the late Sir William Macnaghten, for the evacuation of Afghanistan by the troops, we have the honour to request that you will intimate to the officer commanding at Jellalabad our wish that the troops now at that place should return to India, commencing their march immediately after the receipt of this letter, leaving all guns, the property of Dost Muhammad Khan, with the new governor; as also such stores and baggage as there may not be the means of carrying away, and the provisions in store for our use on arriving at Jellalabad.

Abdool Zhufoor Khan, who is the bearer of this letter, will render you all the assistance in his power. He has been appointed governor of Jellalabad on the part of the existing government.

ELDRED POTTINGER
W.K. ELPHINSTONE

Major-General Sir R. Sale and Captain Macgregor to Major Pottinger and Major-General Elphinstone

Jellalabad, January 9, 1842

We have the honour to acknowledge the receipt of your letter of the 29th ultimo, which you therein state was to be delivered to us by Abdool Zhufoor Khan, appointed governor of this place by the existing powers at Cabool. That communication was not handed to us by him, but by a messenger of his; and though dated 29th December 1841 has only this moment reached us.

We have, at the same time, positive information that Mahomed Akbar Khan has sent a proclamation to all the chiefs in the neighbourhood, urging them to raise their followers for the purpose of intercepting and destroying the force now at Jellalabad. Under these circumstances, we have deemed it our duty to await a further communication from you, which we desire may point out the security which is to be given for our safe march to Peshawur.

R. SALE

G.H. MACGREGOR

Brigadier Wild to Major-General Lumley

Camp, Kowulsur, January 7, 1842

I have the honour to acknowledge the receipt, today, of your letter of the 26th ultimo, and to state in reply that I did acknowledge the receipt of the original instructions which you sent me, on the 20th ultimo. I shall, as desired, have his excellency's orders conveyed to Captain Ponsonby, now residing at Peshawur, to await there the arrival of Major-General Pollock.

My former letters will have informed his excellency the commander-in-chief that I consider an advance through the Khyber Pass, with the means at my disposal – having no other cavalry but a troop of Irregular Cavalry, with some indifferent artillery – as somewhat hazardous and likely to cost many lives; but that I shall run the risk of it if occasion requires it.

From the various information I have obtained, an advance through the Khyber Pass ought not to be attempted, except under favourable circumstances, with a less force than 6,000 men with six guns, besides cavalry, the want of which may be felt immediately after emerging from the western extremity of the pass, beyond Landi Khana, on approaching Dakka; and that it would require a whole corps at Ali Musjid to maintain the command of water, which must be brought to the fort from some distance, and to assist in keeping open the communication if the Afreedees were determined on opposing us; and that it would require two corps more, with some guns, to be posted near Gharri Lala Beg, Luagee and Landi Khana, to maintain the communication open above, and to be sufficiently strong to resist the attacks of the Khyberees.

With reference to Captain Ferris's jezailchee corps, I understand from him that when he left Pesh Boluk he had one wing on duty at Jellalabad, which is still there; about 150 men are at Lalpura, to which place they escorted grain and treasure by the Tatara Pass, and the remainder, consisting, I believe, of about 40, is the only part of his corps that could accompany the brigade.

The Sikhs show such extreme lukewarmness, not to say reluctance, in the co-operation they are required to afford that their assistance in the field, or in keeping open the communication in the Khyber Pass, is in no way to be depended on.

C. F. WILD

Brigadier Wild to General Sir Jasper Nicolls

Camp, Kowulsur, January 8, 1842

I was honoured yesterday afternoon with your Excellency's letter of the 27th ultimo regarding the advance, through the Khyber Pass, of the brigade under my command, and I have never felt so deeply impressed as on the occasion of its perusal, with the difference there is between simply obeying orders and acting on my own responsibility, in a case affecting the lives of thousands, and perhaps the vital interests of the state, though I trust, with the Almighty's help, I shall not be found wanting in firmness and perseverance, when the time for acting may arrive.

In replying yesterday to the deputy adjutant-general's official letter of the 26th December, I stated that, from the information I had obtained from various quarters, the general impression was that an advance through the Khyber Pass, except under favourable circumstances, ought not to be attempted with a less force than 6,000 men, six guns and some cavalry, and mine is wanting of that strength by a complement of one-third. The brigade under the orders of Major-General McCaskill will not probably reach Peshawur before 8th or 10th February, and will not be within reach to support mine, in the event of my advancing now. Should any disaster befall me that brigade would then be placed in a predicament worse even than what mine now stands in.

What the views of government, as to our retaining possession of Jellalabad, may be after our troops evacuate Cabool, which, by a letter received from Captain Pottinger, appears to have been decided upon there, I, of course, know not; but if no immediate danger threatens the force of Sir Robert Sale at Jellalabad, and he can maintain himself there in safety, until Major-General McCaskill's brigade arrive here, our united brigades advancing together would be able to afford Major-General Sir Robert Sale certain and effectual relief, and be prepared also to join his force in carrying on offensive operations if required; whereas, if each brigade in succession were to reach Jellalabad in a crippled state, from having been unable singly to overpower the resistance opposed to its progress, both may arrive there so weakened as to reduce the whole to a state of inefficiency.

The Sikh soldiery, too, is in such a disorganized and insubordinate state that no confidence can be placed in any show of assistance on the part of the Lahore government. The men, as well as their chiefs, are decidedly averse to contribute in any way to the success of our arms. General Avitabile, who paid me a visit this evening on his return from Jamrud, related the two following instances of insubordination which occurred today. He ordered two battalions, which it was intended should co-operate with us, to move out to Jamrud from their lines at Peshawur; they flatly refused and gave him to understand that they intended to return to Lahore. In the next place, he ordered three guns to be taken to Jamrud; but as these were in progress the same Sikh soldiers seized on one of them as they passed in front of their lines and let only the other two proceed. No reliance whatever can therefore be placed on their keeping the communication open in our rear in the event of our advancing, and there is still less chance that they will move onwards with us, even so far as Ali Musjid.

Your Excellency alludes to the firm occupation of Ali Musjid, and Major Craigie says that 'it ought to be occupied by three companies of native infantry, well provisioned and with a good store of ammunition'. Captain Ferris, who was left to garrison that fort when it was first taken, and Captain Mackeson have assured me that in case the Afreedees were decidedly hostile, nothing short of one complete regiment could maintain itself there, as the command of water, which had to be brought to the fort from a considerable distance, could not be secured without a strong garrison. Should I find this to be really the case, it would reduce my strength for ulterior progress very much.

Landi Khana, near the upper or western extremity of the Khyber Pass, to which your Excellency also calls my attention as a suitable position to be occupied, has been represented to me as the most contracted and formidable part of the whole Khyber Pass, and it will be difficult to find in its neighbourhood a position that is not commanded by some near adjoining hill.

There is another position, which has likewise been pointed out to me, between Ali Musjid and Landi Khana, in the vicinity of Gharri Lala Beg and Luagee, as one that ought to be occupied to keep the communication open, but these posts would require to be of such strength to guard against attack that there would not be any troops left to advance after getting through the pass; whilst the greatest difficulty would be to supply them with provisions, as it would, except in the most urgent case, be impossible for us to advance immediately for want of cattle.

We had been informed by the commissariat that the camels we brought with us from Ferozepore had been bound down by an agreement to proceed with us to Jellalabad, on payment of 12 rupees each in advance, a very high rate of hire. Our stores, ammunition and commissariat supplies were all loaded on them, but, to the great annoyance of the political agent, myself and all concerned, the camel owners denied being a party in the agreement; they could not be forced, and neither threats nor the most liberal offers of remuneration could induce above one-fourth of them to move on a step beyond this; nay, these even repent, and are not to be depended upon. Captain Mackeson is now trying to supply the place of camels, for the carriage of grain, etc., with bullocks and ponies, for there is no commissariat officer either with me or at Peshawur to arrange these matters.

I am told that on emerging from the pass beyond Landi Khana, and thence on to Jellalabad, we are likely to feel the want of cavalry for the protection of the cattle.

The troops, I am happy to say, are healthy, though on arriving here they felt fatigued after their long march, for when they came to the crossing of a river, the day that would otherwise have been a halt for them was a harder working day than any other, to unload and load the ferry boats with commissariat stores, ammunition, baggage, etc. I shall, however, be obliged to leave behind me here 30 or 40 sick, most of them men who were brought before the invaliding committee last year, but were not passed because it was thought two or three years' work might still be got out of them.

General Avitabile has repeatedly expatiated on the danger of proceeding through the Khyber Pass with so small a force as the one under my command, and entreated me not to act rashly in the attempt. Major-General Sir Robert Sale, on the other hand, is rather peremptory in his desire that I should hasten on to Jellalabad, but I conceive he could not have been aware of the instructions I received by your Excellency's orders, nor of the hazardous nature of the attempt. I, however, wrote to him yesterday that if he thought of retiring upon Peshawur, I would not then hesitate to advance and to take up position at any cost in the Khyber Pass in order to facilitate his retreat.

C.F. WILD

Brigadier Wild to Major-General Lumley

Camp, Kowulsur, January 9, 1842

I have not yet received your letter of the 30th ultimo, but Captain Mackeson has communicated to me the copy of it which was sent to Mr Clerk.

I had the honour of informing you in my last of the present distribution of Captain Ferris's corps of jezailchees, which would make known to his excellency the commander-in chief how very few men belonging to it remain with him, and out of that number I find that there are about 15 who have not yet recovered from the effects of their wounds, leaving in fact only 25 men fit for duty. Those that were detached as an escort with grain and treasure to Lalpura, as mentioned by me in a former letter, amounting to about 170, have been recalled; their number is supposed to be considerably reduced since.

Captain Ferris has promised me a statement of his corps when that detachment arrives. He has had many desertions of late, both among the men who were detached hence and those at Jellalabad, which he partly attributes to want of pay, they being four months' in arrears, and those who have gone have taken their jezails or rifles with them, which is a serious loss. Captain Ferris has been trying to recruit trustworthy men here to fill up the vacancies in his corps, without success; he does not think the men to be had could be depended upon, or safely trusted with a jezail or ammunition for it; but there is another description of people to be had here, matchlockmen, named Arbabs, on whom some little dependence can be placed. Captain Mackeson has already entertained about three or four of them. They may prove useful, and as Captain Ferris with his adjutant Lieutenant Lukin are both in camp, and understand the language and manners of those people well, I do not think that the Arbabs could be placed under a better superintendence than that of those two officers.

With reference to the arming of our troops for operation in mountain defiles with the weapon of the Afghan 'soldiery', I will consult Captain Mackeson as to how and in what manner they may be obtained.

Captain Pottinger has written to Captain Macgregor, political agent at Jellalabad, a short note dated Cabool, 25th ultimo, confirming the melancholy intelligence of Sir William Macnaghten's murder by Mahomed Akbar Khan, and saying that a treaty had been entered into with the Afghan chiefs for the immediate evacuation of Cabool by the British troops, to retire upon Peshawur; but he adds, as he was closing his letter, that an attack was made upon our cantonments. In consequence of the death and imprisonment of all his seniors in the political department, Captain Pottinger was left at the head of affairs. Subsequent native reports received at Jellalabad say that after Sir

William Macnaghten's murder provisions still continued to be carried to cantonments by the country people, and that it was again quiet.

Nevertheless, Captain Macgregor is most anxious that the force under my command should arrive at Jellalabad, taking it for granted, as it were, that it will do so in perfect safety and be ready for any emergency, without considering that, as soon as we have entered the pass a door closes, as it were, upon our rear, there being no other force close at hand to support our advance or to take advantage thereof for its own benefit; so that if my brigade should have the misfortune to meet with a disaster, Major-General McCaskill's brigade would then stand in a worse predicament even than mine does now, so that the chances are that both brigades would reach Jellalabad in a crippled state one after the other; for the co-operation of our Sikh allies is by no means to be depended upon.

The Sikh troops are in a thorough state of insubordination; they obey only when and as much as they please. Two battalions flatly refused to move out of their lines when ordered, two days ago, by General Avitabile to proceed to Jamrud with a view eventually to co-operate with us, and intimated that it was their intention to return to Lahore; they also laid hold on one out of three guns that were proceeding to Jamrud by the general's orders and conveyed it back to their own lines. Under such circumstances it is evident that we neither can depend on their active co-operation in the field, nor on obtaining the communication open for us in the rear.

The security into which the whole brigade has been lulled by the official announcement that a contract had been entered into by which all the Rewarree camels – those in the employ of the commissariat for the conveyance of ammunition, stores, etc., as well as those hired by individuals – were to continue their services until the force should reach Jellalabad on the further payment, in advance, of 12 rupees each, has been sadly disappointed by the most decided and obstinate refusal of the camel owners in camp to abide by the agreement, or to acknowledge the competency of those who are alleged to have contracted it in their names to do so.

The consequence has been that we have literally been left without carriage of any kind to proceed with, besides the few company's camels that carry the sepoys' camp equipage. Neither liberal promises nor threats could prevail on the camel owners to come to any terms, and after giving the greatest possible annoyance, Captain Mackeson, as a last expedient, offered to purchase them, but only about 300 were secured on those terms yesterday.

The conviction that the agreement must hold good prevented both the political agent, on the part of government, and individuals on their private accounts to make any arrangement to supply the want of carriage for the further progress of the troops towards Jellalabad after reaching Peshawur, so that an immediate advance, except in a case of extreme urgency and leaving almost every necessary article behind us, could not take place; though I hope with the active measures now on foot, this impediment will be removed in two or three days.

Captain Mackeson has not yet received a satisfactory answer from the Afreedee chiefs, to whom terms for allowing us to pass through the Khyber Pass have been offered. They plead divisions among themselves as the cause which renders it impossible for them to give a reply for some days.

The broken limber of the gun (by firing it off the other day) has been substantially repaired.

C.F. WILD

Major-General Sir R. Sale to the Officer Commanding at Peshawur

Jellalabad, January 9, 1842

I have the honour to acknowledge the receipt of your letter of the 27th ultimo, which has only this moment reached me. Captain Mackeson will be able to communicate to you the substance of the important intelligence sent to Captain Macgregor, from Cabool, under date 29th ultimo; with reference to which it is my opinion that you ought to lose no time in advancing on this place, which will enable us either to hold it against any enemy, or in every event to retire in perfectly good order across the Khyber.

R. SALE

PS A letter from Captain Mackeson, of the 3rd instant, mentions that he has obtained four field pieces from General Avitabile, which will be sufficient, I think, for your operations.

Major-General Sir R. Sale to Brigadier Wild

Jellalabad, January 10, 1842

I had the honour, late yesterday evening, to receive yours of the 2nd instant. The postmaster at Peshawur will be best able to explain the delay in the transmission of both this and yours of the 27th ultimo, as well as of that of a private communication of the 16th December from General Sir J. Nicolls, KCB, which also came to hand on the same day, and gave me the first intimation of the circumstance of a separate command being vested in you, which will not merge in mine until you reach Jellalabad.

I have to thank you for the co-operation which you have shown every disposition to afford me, and once more beg to be permitted to press upon your attention the paramount importance, as respects British interests in Afghanistan at this moment, of your appearing with the least practicable delay under the walls of Jellalabad. I shall esteem it a favour to be informed of your progress by every available opportunity.

   R. SALE

Major-General Sir R. Sale to Brigadier Wild

Jellalabad, January 11, 1842

Your letter of the 7th instant I have this moment received, and in reply I can only again repeat that I consider the appearance of your brigade under the walls of Jellalabad would have the effect of restoring confidence at this crisis, and tranquillizing the country on this side of Gundamuck, besides affording the only hope of extricating from a situation, perilous in the extreme, our troops at Cabool.

I am of opinion that your deficiency in cavalry could not be materially felt in such a route as that of the passes of the Khyber. The circumstance of your delay beyond the time when your approach was expected has already produced the effect of inducing all the surrounding chiefs, who had hitherto been faithful, to manifest decided indications of an intention to desert our cause. It has also greatly depressed the spirits of our native soldiers in this garrison, who are anxiously looking for reinforcements and are four months in arrears of pay. We have not a single rupee within these walls, and our ammunition is not sufficient to enable us to fight our way from Jellalabad.

Having been entrusted with a separate command, you are of course the best judge of your own operations, and alone responsible for them, but I must repeat that I consider that the fate and prospects of the British force at Cabool and this place chiefly depend on a speedy support of us.

Should any untoward circumstance occur that would compel me to retire on Peshawur, it would be, after this, impossible to communicate with you, so as to enable you to assist us in our retreat, as your present delay will probably close the route even for single cossids.

   R. SALE

Major-General Sir J.R. Sale to Major-General Lumley

Jellalabad, January 12, 1842

In order that his excellency the commander-in-chief may be in full possession of the exact state of affairs, I have the honour to forward copies of the whole of the correspondence between Brigadier Wild and myself, and have the honour to request you will submit them, together with this letter, to his excellency for perusal.

You will perceive that I had opened this correspondence before I was made aware that Brigadier Wild's command was intended to be separate and independent of mine up to the time of his arrival here.

With reference to the whole of those letters, but especially the last, I have only to remark that, if the brigadier could have marched from Jamrud, even so late as the 7th instant, I cannot doubt that his advance would have kept all the Afghan sirdars around us, who have hitherto been friendly, still true to our interests; and it is probable that the Ghilzie sirdars from Lughman would have separated themselves from the confederacy.

The very contrary effect has been produced by the indefinite delay which he unfortunately announces to me. The confidence in us of even the governor of this place, and of his adherents without, is evidently shaken. They doubt whether we shall ever be reinforced and seemed prepared to leave us; and in case of the force at Cabool coming down in confusion to seek shelter within these walls, it is quite certain that the armed population would rise to a man to intercept them and us. Again, if the brigadier had been able promptly to move on, he would have met with no opposition, excepting in the Khyber Pass, between Jamrud and Dakka, for we had positive information that the people from the latter place to Jellalabad had made arrangements to carry off their families and leave the road clear for the column; but when once the impulse of resistance is given to the armed peasantry, the brigadier will only be able to appear here after contesting every inch of both mountains and plains from Jamrud to this spot.

I regret this delay, which has produced a great depression of spirits amongst the soldiers of this garrison, and beg of you to understand that I pass no judgement on the movements of Brigadier Wild, for which he is alone responsible.

R. SALE

Brigadier Wild to Major-General Lumley

Camp, Kowulsur, January 12, 1842

I have the honour to state, for the information of his excellency the commander-in-chief, that I learnt from Captain Mackeson, who has this moment called upon me, that Captain Macgregor, the political agent at Jellalabad, had received a letter from Captain Pottinger, dated Cabool, the 28th ultimo, written in French.

That makes no mention of any engagement having, as supposed, taken place on the 25th ultimo, but he states that the strength of the cantonment had been considerably weakened by the late Sir William Macnaghten's surrender of some adjoining forts; that the troops had been desired to retire upon Jellalabad as soon as carriage for the sick and wounded should be sent (which was expected in the course of the day) by the Bungiah Pass, but that they would not consent to proceed by that route; that Captain Pottinger also warns Captain Macgregor not to obey an order sent to him by the late envoy to surrender Jellalabad and to retire upon Peshawur, unless it should be reiterated by himself.

Under such circumstances, it may be imperatively required to run the risk of forcing our way through the Khyber Pass, and to advance to the relief of the force at Jellalabad. No friendly forbearance on the part of the Afreedee tribes can any longer be reckoned upon, and it becomes a matter of most serious consideration how to proceed. The best plan, in my opinion, is to make our way through it as speedily as practicable before their vigilance be excited so as to preclude, as well as frustrate, any serious resistance.

The proposed mode of proceeding, subject to such modification as circumstances at the moment may require, is to ascertain in the first instance whether there is any hope of co-operation on the part of the Sikh troops, so as to get a couple of their corps to accompany the brigade to Ali Musjid and to leave them there with a view to maintain the communication open to a certain extent by their occupation of that post. In this case, I would take up a new position with the brigade in the morning of the day when it was intended to move about six miles in advance of the present camp, close to the entrance of the pass at Jamrud; and after the men shall have taken their meals comfortably during the day, I would order them in the evening to get under arms at as short a notice, and with as little noise, as possible and proceed at once to Ali Musjid, a distance of eight miles, in the dark, leaving, with a few exceptions of the most indispensable articles, all the tents and baggage behind them. and if successful so far, to push on forthwith to the end of the pass to Lalpura, where it will be necessary to wait a day or two for the arrival of the camp equipage, which could be forwarded thither by the Tatara Pass, as the want of it would be much felt at this inclement season of the year when much rain may be expected.

Part of the treasure, in the event of such a move, will have to be left behind, but I shall endeavour to take all the ammunition with me. Independent of the want of sufficient carriage, it will be impossible to take supplies of provision in any large quantity in a movement requiring celerity and secrecy, and one which, if delayed too long, may no longer be practicable. Nevertheless, Captain Mackeson, who entirely concurs in the above measure, still holds a communication open with the Mahks, or Afreedee chiefs, and seems anxious to avoid any collision with them until their definitive answer to the terms offered shall have been received.

Very few camels, and the strongest only, can be taken; their liability to fall and obstruct a passage, and the slowness of their progress over stony roads, might defeat our object. For the same reason, Captain Mackeson will endeavour to secure the loan of some elephants from General Avitabile to carry the guns through the pass, lest the restiveness of the horses, or some other untoward obstacle, should cause some breakage and delay in consequence. If only Major-General McCaskill's brigade were near at hand, I should feel a confidence as to the maintenance of an open communication in the rear, which 10,000 Sikh troops could never inspire.

The disasters at Cabool are well known at Peshawur, with considerable exaggeration, and have much increased the insolence of its inhabitants towards us.

C.F. WILD

Major-General Sir Robert Sale to Major-General Lumley

Jellalabad, January 13, 1842

I beg to acquaint you, for the information of his excellency the commander-in-chief, that Assistant Surgeon Brydon, a few hours since, arrived at this place wounded and has reported that, on the faith of a treaty, our troops left Cabool on or about the 6th instant. They were treacherously attacked on the road by overwhelming numbers, and from the nature of his recital there is reason to expect that he is the only one of the fugitives that we shall ever see alive.

Relying on his excellency the commander-in-chief's promise to relieve us as soon as possible, I have resolved on the most determined defence of this place; but if his excellency will understand that the parapets are not cannon-proof, and that we may expect to be besieged immediately by the Afghans, aided by a considerable artillery, I feel that this short statement is the strongest appeal I can make for succour.

R. SALE

Extracts from the Diaries of Lieutenant Vincent Eyre and Lady Florentia Sale

Lady Florentia Sale (1790–1853)

In making the assumption that Assistant Surgeon Brydon may be 'the only one of the fugitives we shall ever see alive', Brigadier Sale was presuming the loss of life not only of the entire garrison but also of his wife, daughter and son-in-law. To this personal tragedy he makes no reference.

However, he was mercifully wrong. ... As shall become clear from the pages that follow, a number of the fleeing army and their followers were taken hostage along the route. This small band was moved around the region, in dread fear of their lives, for eight months before being reunited with the surviving force at Jellalabad.

Two of these people kept diaries: Lieutenant Vincent Eyre and Lady Sale. Their accounts were both published in London on their return and were the first description available to the public of the depth of horror of what had occurred.

Lt Eyre's version was edited by his brother and is sharp in its criticism of the handling of the military enterprise. Lady Sale's story is not only critical but also a personal and moving account of the survival of herself and her daughter in one of the most appalling captivities in history. Their story ends with the emotional meeting with her husband.

The retreat from Cabool – the third day. In the central group: Lady Sale, who was wounded in the arm on this day; her son-in-law, Lieutenant Sturt, receiving his fatal wound; and Major-General Elphinstone, with his mameluke sword

From Lieutenant Eyre's Diary

December 23, 1841

The bodyguard had only got a few hundred yards from the gate in their progress to the scene of conference, when they suddenly faced about and came galloping back, several shots being fired at them in their retreat. Lieutenant Le Geyt, in passing through the gate, exclaimed that the envoy [Sir William Macnaghten] had been carried off, and it was believed that, finding his men would not advance to the rescue, he came back for assistance.

But the intelligence he brought, instead of rousing our leaders to instant action, seemed to paralyse their faculties; and, although it was evident that our envoy had been basely entrapped, if not actually murdered, before our very gate, and though even now crowds of Afghans, horse and foot, were seen passing and repassing to and fro in hostile array, between Mahomed's fort and the place of meeting, not a gun was opened upon them; not a soldier was stirred from his post; no sortie was apparently even thought of; treachery was allowed to triumph in open day; the murder of a British envoy was perpetrated in the face of and within musket-shot of a British army; and not only was no effort made to avenge the dastardly deed, but the body was left lying on the plain to be mangled and insulted, and was finally carried off to be paraded in the public market by a ruffianly mob of fanatical barbarians.

Intense was the anxiety and wretched the suspense felt by all during the rest of the day. A number of Afghans, who were trafficking in cantonments at the time of the conference, on hearing the report of firearms in that direction, endeavoured to escape, but were detained by the officer at the gate. No certain tidings regarding the envoy could be obtained; many confidently affirmed that he was alive and unharmed in Mahomed's fort; but Lieutenant Warren stoutly maintained that he had kept his eye upon Sir William from the moment of his leaving the gate, and had distinctly seen him fall to the ground and the Afghans hacking at his body. The agony of his poor wife during this dread interval of suspense may be imagined.

December 24, 1841

The fate of the envoy and his three companions remained a mystery until the arrival of a note from Captain Conolly notifying his death and that of Captain Trevor, and the safety of Captains Lawrence and Mackenzie.

The two latter officers had been that morning escorted to a conference of chiefs at the house of Nawab Zeman Khan, where the late envoy's conduct was severely commented on; but his death was nevertheless lamented. The treaty was again discussed; and, after a few alterations and additions had been made, it was sent to General Elphinstone, with an explanation of the breach of faith which had cost the envoy his life.

General Elphinstone now requested Major Pottinger to assume the office of political agent and adviser, which, though still suffering greatly from his wound, and incapacitated from active bodily exertion, that gallant officer's strict sense of public duty forbade him to decline, although he plainly perceived our affairs to be so irretrievably ruined as to render the distinction anything but enviable, or likely to improve his hardly earned fame.

The additional clauses in the treaty now proposed for our renewed acceptance were, first, that we should leave behind all our guns, excepting six; second, that we should immediately give up all our treasures; third, that the hostages should be all exchanged for married men, with their wives and families. The difficulties of Major Pottinger's position will be readily perceived, when it is borne in mind that he had before him the most conclusive evidence of the late envoy's ill-advised intrigue with Mahomed Akbar Khan, in direct violation of that very treaty, which was now once more tendered for consideration.

December 25, 1841

A more cheerless Christmas Day perhaps never dawned upon British soldiers in a strange land; and the few whom the force of habit urged to exchange the customary greetings of the season did so with countenances and in tones indicative of anything but merriment. At night there was an alarm, and the drum beat to arms, but nothing occurred of any consequence.

December 26, 1841

Letters were received from Captain Mackeson, political agent at Peshawur, announcing the march of strong reinforcements from India. An offer was made by Mahomed Oosman Khan to escort us all safe to Peshawur for five lacs of rupees; and shortly after this the Naib Ameer arrived, with a verbal agreement to certain amendments which had been proposed in the treaty by Major Pottinger. He was accompanied by a Cashmeer merchant and several Hindoo shroffs, for the purpose of negotiating bills to the amount of 14 lacs of rupees payable to the several chiefs on the promise of the late envoy.

Major Pottinger being altogether averse to the payment of this money, and indeed strongly opposed to any treaty binding the Indian government to a course of policy which it might find inconvenient to adopt, a council of war was convened by the general, consisting of himself, Brigadiers Shelton and Anquetil, Colonel Chambers, Captain Bellow, Assistant Quarter-Master General, and Captain Grant, Assistant Adjutant-General.

In the presence of this council, Major Pottinger declared his conviction that no confidence could be placed in any treaty formed with the Afghan chiefs; that under such circumstances, to bind the hands of government by promising to evacuate the country and to restore the deposed Ameer – and to waste moreover so much public money merely to save our own lives and property – would be inconsistent with the duty we owed our country and the government we served; and that the only honourable course would be either to hold out to the last at Cabool, or to force our immediate retreat to Jellalabad.

This, however, the officers composing the council, one and all, declared to be impracticable, owing to the want of provisions the surrender of the surrounding forts and the insuperable difficulties of the road at the present season. They therefore deemed it preferable to pay any sum of money rather than sacrifice the whole force in a hopeless prolongation of hostilities. It was accordingly determined, *nem. con.*, that Major Pottinger should at once renew the negotiations which had been commenced by Sir William Macnaghten, and that the sums promised to the chiefs by that functionary previous to his murder should be paid.

Major Pottinger's objections being thus overruled, the tendered treaty was forthwith accepted, and a requisition was made for the release of Captain Lawrence, whose presence was necessary to prepare the bills on India. Four married hostages, with their wives and children, being required by the chiefs, a circular was sent round to ascertain if that number would volunteer to remain, a salary of 2,000 rupees per month being guaranteed to each as an inducement.

Such, however, was the horror entertained of Afghan treachery since the late tragical occurrence that some officers went so far as to say they would sooner shoot their wives at once than commit them to the charge of men who had proved themselves devoid of common honour and humanity. There were, in fact, but one or two who consented to stay if the general considered that by so doing they would benefit the public service.

December 27, 1841

The chiefs were informed that it was contrary to the usages of war to give up ladies as hostages, and that the general could not consent to an arrangement which would brand him with perpetual disgrace in his own country.

December 29, 1841

The Naib Ameer came in from the city with Captain Lawrence and the shroffs, and the bills were prepared without further delay. Captains Drummond, Walsh, Warburton and Webb, having been accepted as hostages, were sent to join Captains Conolly and Airey at the house of Nawab Zeman Khan. A portion of the sick and wounded, amongst whom was Lieutenant Haughton of the Goorkha regiment, were likewise conveyed to the city and placed under the protection of the chiefs. Three of the Shah's guns, with the greater portion of our treasure, were made over during the day, much to the evident disgust of the soldiery.

December 30, 1941

The remainder of the sick went into the city. Lieutenant Evans, Her Majesty's 44th Foot, was placed in command, and Dr Campbell, 54th Native Infantry, with Dr Berwick of the Mission, was in medical charge of the whole. Two more of the Shah's guns were given up. It snowed hard the whole day.

A crowd of armed Ghilzies and Ghazees took up a threatening position close to the eastern gate, and even attempted to force an entrance into cantonments. Much annoyance was daily experienced from these people, who were in the habit of plundering the peaceable dealers, who flocked in from the city with grain and forage, the moment they issued from the cantonments; they even committed frequent assaults on our sepoys, and orders to fire on them on such occasions were repeatedly solicited in vain, although it was well known that the chiefs themselves advised us to do so, and that the general had given Brigadier Shelton positive instructions to that effect whenever circumstances might render it advisable.

The consequence was that our soldiers were daily constrained to endure the most insulting and contemptuous taunts and treatment from fellows whom a single charge of bayonets would have scattered like chaff, but who were emboldened by the apparent tameness of our troops, which they doubtless attributed to the want of common pluck rather than to the restraints of discipline. Captains Mackenzie and Skinner obtained their release this evening, the latter officer having, since the outbreak of the rebellion, passed through some curious adventures in the disguise of an Afghan female.

January 5, 1842

Affairs continued in the same unsettled state until this date. The chiefs postponed our departure from day to day on divers pretexts. It had been agreed that Nawab Jubbar Khan should escort us to Jellalabad with about 2,000 followers, who were to be entertained for that purpose.

It is supposed that, up to the very last, the majority of chiefs doubted the reality of our intention to depart; and many, fearful of the civil discords for which our retreat would be the signal, would have gladly detained us at Cabool. Attempts were made continually by Akbar Khan to wean the Hindoostanees from their allegiance and to induce them to desert. Numerous cautions were received from various well-wishers to place no confidence in the professions of the chiefs, who had sworn together to accomplish our entire destruction.

Shah Shuja himself sent more than one solemn warning and, finding we were bent on taking our own course, used his utmost endeavours to persuade Lady Macnaghten to take advantage of his protection in the Bala Hissar. He also appealed to Brigadier Anquetil, who commanded the Shah's force, 'if it were well to forsake him in the hour of need, and to deprive him of the aid of that force, which he had hitherto been taught to consider as his own?' All was however unavailing. The general and his council of war had determined that go we must, and go we accordingly did.

In the foregoing pages I have offered what I honestly believe to be a faithful narration of the dismal train of events which preceded the evacuation of Cabool and the abandonment of Shah Shuja by the British army. In taking a retrospective view of those unprecedented occurrences, it is evident that our reverses may be mainly attributed to a lack of ordinary foresight and penetration on the part of the chief military and civil authorities on their first entering on the occupation of this country, a country whose innumerable fortified strongholds and difficult mountain passes – in the hands of a proud and warlike population, never really subdued nor reconciled to our rule, though unable to oppose the march of a disciplined army through their land – ought to have induced a more than common degree of vigilance and circumspection in making adequate provision against any such popular outbreak as might have been anticipated, and did actually occur.

But, instead of applying his undeniable talents to the completion of that conquest which gained him an illustrious title and a wide renown, Lord Keane contented himself with the superficial success which attended his progress through a country hitherto untraversed by a European army since the classic days of Alexander the Great. He hurried off, with too great eagerness, to enjoy the applause which awaited him in England, and left to his successors the far more arduous task of securing in their grasp the unwieldy prize, of which he had obtained the nominal possession.

On his return to India, Lord Keane took with him a large portion of the Bengal force with which he had arrived at Cabool; the whole of the Bombay troops made a simultaneous homeward movement; and the army, with which Lord Keane had entered Afghanistan was thus reduced to a miserable moiety, before any steps had been taken to guard against surprise by the erection of a stronghold on the approved principles of modern warfare, or by the establishment of a line of military posts to keep open our communications with India, on which country the army must necessarily for a long time have been entirely dependent for the munitions of war.

The distance from Cabool to Ferozepore, our nearest Indian station, is about 600 miles. Between Cabool and Peshawur occur the stupendous and dangerous defiles of Khoord Cabool, Tezeen, Puree Duree, Jugduluk and Kyber, throughout whose whole extent food and forage are procurable only at long intervals, and even then with much difficulty.

From Peshawur to Ferozepore is the Punjab, or country of the Sikhs, traversed by five great rivers and occupied by a powerful nation on whose pacific professions no reliance could be placed. Along this extended line of communication Lord Keane established but one small solitary post, in the fort of Ali Musjid in the heart of the Khyber Pass. He left behind him, in fact, an army whose isolated position and reduced strength offered the strongest possible temptation to a proud and restless race to rally their scattered tribes in one grand effort to regain their lost independence.

In Lord Keane's successors may be seen the same disposition to be too easily satisfied with the outward semblance of tranquillity. Another brigade was ere long withdrawn from a force already insufficient for any great emergency; nor was their position for holding in subjection a vanquished people much improved by their establishment in an ill-situated and ill-constructed cantonment, with their commissariat stores separated from their lines of defence. To the latter mentioned error may be mainly attributed the evacuation of Cabool and the destruction of the army, for there can be no doubt that, notwithstanding all the difficulties of our position, and the incompetence of our commanders, had the cantonments been well supplied with provisions, the troops could have easily held out until the arrival of reinforcements from India.

The real cause of our retreat was, beyond all question, famine. We were not driven, but starved, out of Cabool; and although, in my relation of our military transactions, I have been compelled by a regard to truth unwillingly to record proceedings which must be condemned by all, I do not the less feel most sensibly that every allowance ought in common justice to be made for men who, from the very commencement of the conflict, saw the combined horrors of starvation and a rigorous winter frowning in their face; no succours within reach; their retreat cut off; and all their sanguinary efforts either altogether fruitless, or at best deferring for a few short days the ruin which on every side threatened to overwhelm them.

In connection with this subject, I may be excused for quoting, in conclusion, the powerful reasoning of a recent writer in the *Bombay Times*:

> When a soldier finds that his every movement is directed by a mastermind; that, when he is apparently thrust into the greatest danger, he finds, in truth, his greatest security; that his march to engage an apparently superior force is not a wild sacrifice, but the result of a well-calculated plan, when he knows that, however appearances may be, he is sure to come off with honour, for his brethren in arms are already in progress to assist him and will not fail to be forthcoming at the hour appointed; when he sees that there is a watchful eye over him, providing for all his wants, assisting him to overcome all his difficulties, and enabling him to reap the fruit of all his successes; when he finds that even retreat is but a preparation for victory, and, as if guided by Providence, all his movements, though to him incomprehensible, are sure to prove steps to some great end; when the soldier finds this, he rises and lies down in security, and there is no danger which he will not brave.
>
> But when, in everything they undertake, they find the reverse of the picture I have drawn; when they are marched, as they imagine to glory, but find it is only to slaughter; when even victory brings no fruit, and retreat they discover to be flight; when the support they hope for comes not, and they find their labours to be without end or purpose; when the provisions they look for daily are issued to them no more, and they see all their efforts paralysed; when an army of thousands finds itself delivered, bound hand and foot, into the hands of a man without system, foresight or military knowledge enough for a sergeant of police, the stoutest heart will fail, the bravest sink; for the soldier knows that, do what he will, his efforts can only end in ruin and dishonour.

From Lady Sale's Diary

Thursday, January 6, 1842

We marched from Cabool. The advanced guard consisted of the 44th Queen's, 4th Irregular Horse and Skinner's Horse, two horse artillery 6-pounder guns, Sappers and Miners, Mountain Train and the late envoy's escort. The main body included the 5th and 37th Native Infantry (the latter in charge of treasure) Anderson's Horse, the Shah's 6th Regiment and two horse artillery 6-pounder guns. The rearguard was composed of the 54th Native Infantry, 5th Cavalry and two 6-pounder horse artillery guns. The force consisted of about 4,500 fighting men and 12,000 followers.

The troops left cantonments both by the rear gate and the breach to the right of it, which had been made yesterday by throwing down part of the rampart to form a bridge over the ditch. All was confusion from before daylight. The day was clear and frosty; the snow nearly a foot deep on the ground; the thermometer was considerably below freezing point.

By eight o'clock a great part of the baggage was outside the cantonments. It was fully expected that we would have to fight our way out of them, although terms had been entered into with the sirdar for our safe escort. Bills were granted on India for 14½ lacs of rupees, by the political authority (Major Pottinger) to the Cabool shroffs, to be paid to the following sirdars, who were, on their part, to protect the force as far as Peshawur:

- Mahomed Zeman Shah Khan, three lacs
- Amen Oollah Khan, six lacs
- Khan Shireen Khan, head of the Kuzzilbashes, two lacs
- Mahomed Akbar Khan, one lac
- Oosman Khan, two lacs
- Ghilzie chiefs, half a lac

We started at about half-past nine a.m. The advance party were not molested; there might have been 50 or 100 Afghans collected about the gateway to witness our departure. The ladies, collectively speaking, were placed with the advance, under the charge of the escort, but Mrs Sturt and I rode up to Captain Hay and mixed ourselves with his troopers.

The progress was very slow; for the first mile was not accomplished under two and a half hours. There was only one small bridge over the nullah, which is eight feet broad, but deep, situ-ated about 50 yards from cantonments.

Great stress had been laid on the necessity of a bridge over the Cabool River, about half a mile from the cantonments. In vain had Sturt represented over and over again that, as the river was perfectly fordable, it was a labour of time and inutility: with snow a foot deep, the men must get their feet wet. However, as usual, every sensible proposition was overruled; and Sturt was sent long before daylight to make the bridge with gun carriages. They could not be placed overnight, as the Afghans would have carried them off. He had therefore to work for hours up to his hips in water, with the comfortable assurance that, when his unprofitable task was finished, he could not hope for dry clothes until the end of the march; and immediately on quitting the water they were all frozen stiff. I do not mention this as an individual grievance, but to show the inclemency of the weather and the general misery sustained.

The bullocks had great difficulty in dragging these gun carriages through the snow, and when the bridge was made it was proved to be an unnecessary expense of time and labour. The baggage might have forded the river with great ease, a little above the bridge, where it was not deep. Mrs Sturt and I rode with the horsemen through the river, in preference to attempting the rattling bridge of planks laid across the gun carriages; but the camp followers determined not to go through the water, and jostled for their turns to go over the bridge. This delay was the origin of the day's misfortune, which involved the loss of nearly all the baggage and the greater part of the commissariat stores.

The troops had been on half rations during the whole of the siege: this consisted of half a seer of wheat per diem, with melted ghee or dhal, for fighting men; and for camp followers, for some time, a quarter of a seer of wheat or barley. Our cattle, public and private, had long subsisted on the twigs and bark of the trees. From the commencement of negotiations with the chiefs, atta, barley and bhoosa were brought in in considerable quantities; the former selling at from two to four seers per rupee, and the latter from seven to ten; but neither ourselves nor our servants benefited by this arrangement: it came to the commissariat for the troops.

The poorer camp followers had latterly subsisted on such animals (camels, ponies, etc.) as had died from starvation. The men had suffered much from overwork and bad feeding, also from want of firing; for when all the wood in store was expended, the chiefs objected to our cutting down any more of the fruit trees, and their wishes were complied with. Wood, both public and private, was stolen: when ours was gone, we broke up boxes, chests of drawers, etc., and our last dinner and breakfast at Cabool were cooked with the wood of a mahogany dining table.

When the advance had proceeded about a mile, an order was brought for a return to cantonments, as Mahomed Zeman Shah Khan had written to say the chiefs were not ready; but shortly afterwards a counter-order arrived to proceed without loss of time.

When the rearguard left cantonments, they were fired upon from the cantonment that was then filled with Afghans. The servants, who were not concerned in the plunder, all threw away their loads and ran off. Private baggage, commissariat and ammunition were nearly annihilated at one fell swoop. The whole road was covered with men, women and children lying down in the snow to die. The only baggage we saved was Mrs Sturt's bedding, on which the ayah rode, and keeping her close to us, it was saved.

The mission compound was first vacated: and when the force from thence came into cantonments in order to pass through them, it was immediately filled with Afghans, who, in like manner, occupied the cantonments as our troops went out.

It was the general's original intention to halt at Begramee, close to the Loghur River, and about five miles from Cabool (re-iterated was the advice of our Afghan friends – alas, how little heeded! – to push on at all risks through the Khoord Cabool the first day); but the whole country being a swamp encrusted with ice, we went on about a mile further and halted at about 4 p.m. There were no tents, save two or three small palls that arrived. All scraped away the snow as best they might to make a place to lie down on.

The evening and night were intensely cold: no food for man or beast procurable, except a few handfuls of bhoosa, for which we paid from five to ten rupees. Captain Johnson, in our great distress, kindly pitched a small pall over us: but it was dark, and we had few pegs; the wind blew in under the sides, and I felt myself gradually stiffening. I left the bedding, which was occupied by Mrs Sturt and her husband, and doubled up my legs in a straw chair of Johnson's, covering myself with my posteen. Mr Mein and the ayah fully occupied the remainder of the space. We only went in all six miles and had to abandon two horse artillery guns on the road. We were also much delayed by the bullocks that dragged the planks, in case the Loghur bridge should have been destroyed. We had, however, positive information that it was all right; and so it proved.

Previous to leaving cantonments, as we had to abandon most of our property, Sturt was anxious to save a few of his most valuable books and to try the experiment of sending them to a friend in the city. Whilst he selected these, I found, amongst the ones thrown aside, Campbell's poems, which opened at *Hohenlinden*; and, strange to say, one verse actually haunted me day and night:

> Few, few shall part where many meet,
> The snow shall be their winding sheet,
> And every turf beneath their feet
> Shall be a soldier's sepulchre.

I am far from being a believer in presentiments, but this verse is never absent from my thoughts. Heaven forbid that our fears should be realized! But we have commenced our retreat so badly that we may reasonably have our doubts regarding the finale. Nearly all Hopkins's corps, the Shah's 6th, deserted from this place; as also the Shah's Sappers and Miners, 250 in number. We afterwards heard that 400 of Hopkins's men went back to Cabool the next day.

Friday, January 7, 1982

Yesterday's rearguard did not get up to our bivouac till two this morning, as there was no attempt to form any lines. As stragglers came up we heard them shouting out, to know where their corps were; and the general reply was that no one knew anything about it.

During last night, or rather towards the morning, there was an alarm. Had it proved the enemy, we were perfectly defenceless; fortunately it was only camp followers, etc.

At daylight we found several men frozen to death, amongst whom was Mr Conductor Macgregor.

The reason the rearguard were so late was that they did not leave cantonments till sunset. Previous to their quitting them the Afghans had entered and set fire to all the public and private buildings, after plundering them of their contents. The whole of our valuable magazine was looted by the mob; and they burned the gun carriages to procure the iron. Some fighting took place between the Afghans and our Sipahees. About 50 of the 54th were killed and wounded; and Cornet Hardyman, of the 5th Cavalry, was killed. A great deal of baggage and public property was abandoned in cantonments, or lost on the road; amongst which were two horse artillery 6-pounders, as before mentioned.

The officers of the rearguard report that the road is strewn with baggage and that numbers of men, women and children are left on the roadside to perish. Captain Boyd's office accounts, to the amount of several lakhs of rupees, have been lost.

Two or three small tents came up today. The men were half-frozen; having bivouacked all night in the snow, without a particle of food or bedding, or wood to light a fire.

At half-past seven the advance guard moved off. No order was given; no bugle sounded. It had much difficulty in forcing its way ahead of the baggage and camp followers; all of whom had proceeded in advance as soon as it was light. Amongst them there were many Sipahees; and discipline was clearly at an end. If asked why they were not with their corps, one had a lame foot, another could not find his regiment, another had lost his musket: any excuse to run off.

The whole of what little baggage was left was not off the ground ere the enemy appeared and plundered all they could lay their hands on.

As the Mountain Train, consisting of three 3-pounders dragged by yaboos and mules, was passing a small fort close to our back ground, a party of Afghans sallied out and captured the whole. Scarcely any resistance was offered on the part of our troops, and the syces immediately absconded. Brigadier Anquetil and Lieutenant Green rallied the men and retook the guns; but they were obliged to abandon them as the 44th, whose duty it was to guard them, very precipitately made themselves scarce; but this was not done until Anquetil and Green had spiked them with their own hands, amid the gleaming sabres of the enemy. As the troops advanced on their road, the enemy increased considerably on both flanks and greatly annoyed the centre and rear.

It was the general's intention to proceed through the Khoord Cabool Pass to Khoord Cabool; and it was not above 1 p.m. when the advance arrived at Bootkhak, having only come five miles. It was with dismay we heard the order to halt.

We left Cabool with five and a half days' rations to take us to Jellalabad, and no forage for cattle, nor hope of procuring any on the road. By these unnecessary halts we diminished our provisions; and having no cover for officers or men, they are perfectly paralysed with the cold. The snow was more than a foot deep. Here, again, did evil counsel beset the general: his principal officers and staff objecting to a further advance and Captain Grant, in whom he had much confidence, assured him that if he proceeded he risked the safety of the army!

On our arrival at Bootkhak, the enemy had very greatly increased around our position; and we heard that Mahomed Akbar Khan was with them. Scarcely any baggage of either officers or men now remained. In a very small pall of Johnson's we slept nine, all touching each other. We were also indebted to Johnson and Troup for food. They had a few Cabool cakes and some tea, which they kindly shared with us.

During this short march we were obliged to spike and abandon two other 6-pounders, the horses not having strength sufficient to drag them on. We have only two horse artillery guns left, with scarcely any ammunition.

Again no ground was marked out for the troops. Three-fourths of the Sipahees are mixed up with the camp followers, and know not where to find the headquarters of their corps.

Snow still lies a foot deep on the ground. No food for man or beast; and even water from the river close at hand difficult to obtain, as our people were fired on in fetching it.

Numbers of unfortunates have dropped, benumbed with cold, to be massacred by the enemy; yet so bigoted are our rulers that we are still told that the sirdars are faithful, that Mahomed Akbar Khan is our friend! etc., etc.; and the reason they wish us to delay is that they may send their troops to clear the passes for us! That they will send them there can be no doubt; for everything is occurring just as was foretold to us before we set out.

Between Begramee and Bootkhak, a body of the enemy's horse charged down into the column (immediately after the 5th and 37th had passed) and succeeded in carrying off an immense quantity of baggage and a number of camels, without experiencing the least resistance.

Saturday, January 8, 1842

At sunrise no order had been issued for the march, and the confusion was fearful. The force was perfectly disorganized, nearly every man paralysed with cold, so as to be scarcely able to hold his musket or move. Many frozen corpses lay on the ground. The Sipahees burnt their caps, accoutrements and clothes to keep themselves warm. Some of the enemy appearing in rear of our position, the whole of the camp followers rushed to the front; every man, woman, and child seizing all the cattle that fell in their way, whether public or private.

The ground was strewn with boxes of ammunition, plate and property of various kinds. A cask of spirits on the ground was broached by the artillerymen, and, no doubt, by other Europeans. Had the whole been distributed fairly to the men, it would have done them good: as it was, they became too much excited.

The enemy soon assembled in great numbers. Had they made a dash at us, we could have offered no resistance, and all would have been massacred.

After very great exertions on the part of commanding officers, portions of their corps were got together. The 44th, headed by Major Thain, drove the enemy off to a short distance and took up a position on a commanding height. The cavalry were also employed. Bullets kept whizzing by us, as we sat on our horses for hours. The artillerymen were now fully primed, by having had some brandy given them from the 54th's mess stores, which were being distributed to any one who would take them. They mounted their horses and, with the best feeling in the world, declared that they were ashamed at our inactivity and vowed they would charge the enemy. Captain Nicholl, their immediate commandant, came up, abused them as drunkards and talked of punishment: not the way, under such circumstances, to quiet tipsy men.

They turned to Sturt shortly after their own officer had left them, having showered curses and abuse on them, which had irritated them dreadfully. Sturt told them they were fine fellows and had ever proved themselves such during the siege; but that their lives were too valuable to be risked at such a moment; but, if need were, and their services were required, he would himself go with them. This, in a certain degree, restrained their ardour; yet still they kept on talking valiantly.

These men listened the more readily to Sturt because they knew him well: he was daily and hourly in the batteries with them, encouraging them by being ever the foremost in the post of danger; and on those dreadfully cold nights during the siege, whilst there was a bottle of brandy to be had at any price, after his own small store was expended, he gave those men on duty each one glass to warm and cheer them – a comfort they fully appreciated as they had long been without what was now become necessary, though it is in general the soldier's bane.

For myself, whilst I sat for hours on my horse in the cold, I felt very grateful for a tumbler of sherry, which at any other time would have made me very unlady-like, but now merely warmed me, and appeared to have no more strength in it than water. Cups full of sherry were given to young children three- and four-years-old without in the least affecting their heads.

When Major Thain took command of the 44th, he took part of the 37th Native Infantry with him. The 44th lines were nearest to the men who were firing into our camp; which was only saved by the promptness of Thain and Lawrence, who brought up the escort at a trot in the direction of the firing. He had to pass to the right of the 44th, and there he found about 150 of that regiment falling into their ranks. Major Thain was about 200 yards in advance, apparently reconnoitring the enemy, who were creeping up under cover of the ravines and hillocks and keeping up a desultory fire on our camp.

About this time a company of the 37th Native Infantry formed on Lawrence's right, and on Thain making a signal all moved forward and drove off the enemy in good style. Anderson's Horse were formed on the opposite face of the camp, with orders to keep back the camp followers, who were rushing towards the entrance of the pass. Major Thain appears to have acted on the spur of the moment; which is the only reason I can assign for his commanding the 44th. Lawrence was not under anyone's orders; the general, before quitting cantonments, told him that his escort would be an independent body.

I am by no means certain that our chiefs pursued the wisest course. Had they, when the enemy first appeared, showed a good front and dashed at them, they would probably all have scampered off as fast as they could. The Afghans never stand a charge.

The general and Major Pottinger soon discovered that Mahomed Akbar Khan was there and entered into communication with him. He agreed to protect the troops on condition that he should receive hereafter 15,000 rupees; and that Pottinger, Lawrence and Mackenzie should be given over to him as hostages for General Sale's evacuation of Jellalabad; but that the troops should not proceed further than Tezeen until information be received of the march of the troops from that place. These disgraceful propositions were readily assented to, and the three officers went off to the sirdar.

Captain Lawrence received a note from Conolly telling him to be cautious, to put ourselves as little as possible in Akbar's power, and above all things to push on as fast as we could. But this note did not arrive until the conference was over and all points adjusted.

We commenced our march at about midday, the 5th Native Infantry in front. The troops were in the greatest state of disorganization: the baggage was mixed in with the advanced guard; and the camp followers all pushed ahead in their precipitate flight towards Hindoostan.

Sturt, my daughter, Mr Mein and I got up to the advance; and Mr Mein was pointing out to us the spots where the 1st brigade was attacked, and where he, Sale, etc., were wounded. We had not proceeded half a mile when we were heavily fired upon. Chiefs rode with the advance, and desired us to keep close to them. They certainly desired their followers to shout to the people on the height not to fire: they did so, but quite ineffectually. These chiefs certainly ran the same risk we did; but I verily believe many of these persons would individually sacrifice themselves to rid their country of us.

After passing through some very sharp firing, we came upon Major Thain's horse, which had been shot through the loins. When we were supposed to be in comparative safety, poor Sturt rode back (to see after Thain I believe); his horse was shot under him and before he could rise from the ground he received a severe wound in the abdomen. It was with great difficulty he was held upon a pony by two people and brought into camp at Khoord Cabool.

The pony Mrs Sturt rode was wounded in the ear and neck. I had fortunately only one ball in my arm; three others passed through my posteen near the shoulder without doing me any injury. The party that fired on us were not above 50 yards from us, and we owed our escape to urging our horses on as fast as they could go over a road where, at any other time, we should have walked our horses very carefully.

The main attack of the enemy was on the column, baggage and rearguard; and fortunate it was for Mrs Sturt and myself that we kept with the chiefs. Would to God that

Sturt had done likewise and not gone back.

The ladies were mostly travelling in kajawas and were mixed up with the baggage and column in the pass; here they were heavily fired on. Many camels were killed. On one camel were, in one kajawa, Mrs Boyd and her youngest boy Hugh; and in the other Mrs Mainwaring and her infant, scarcely three months old, and Mrs Anderson's eldest child. This camel was shot. Mrs Boyd got a horse to ride; and her child was put on another behind a man who was shortly after unfortunately killed, and the child was carried off by the Afghans. Mrs Mainwaring, less fortunate, took her own baby in her arms. Mary Anderson was carried off in the confusion.

Meeting with a pony laden with treasure, Mrs Mainwaring endeavoured to mount and sit on the boxes, but they upset; and in the hurry pony and treasure were left behind. The unfortunate lady pursued her way on foot, until after a time an Afghan asked her if she was wounded and told her to mount behind him. This apparently kind offer she declined, being fearful of treachery; alleging as an excuse that she could not sit behind him on account of the difficulty of holding her child when so mounted. This man shortly after snatched her shawl off her shoulders and left her to her fate. Mrs Mainwaring's sufferings were very great, and she deserves much credit for having preserved her child through these dreadful scenes. She not only had to walk a considerable distance with her child in her arms through the deep snow, but had also to pick her way over the bodies of the dead, dying and wounded, both men and cattle, and constantly to cross the streams of water, wet up to the knees, pushed and shoved about by men and animals, the enemy keeping up a sharp fire, and several persons being killed close to her. She, however, got safe to camp with her child, but had no opportunity to change her clothes; and I know from experience that it was many days ere my wet habit became thawed and can fully appreciate her discomforts.

Mrs Bourke, little Seymour Stoker and his mother, and Mrs Cunningham, soldiers' wives and the child of a man of the 13th, have been carried off. The rear was protected by the 44th and 37th; but as they neared the pass, the enemy, concealed behind rocks, increased their fire considerably upon them. The companies that had been skirmishing on the flanks of the rearguard closed in; and they slowly entered the pass, keeping up a heavy fire on the assailants, who had by this time got amongst the straggling camp followers and Sipahees.

Owing to a halt having taken place in front, the pass was completely choked up; and for a considerable time the 44th were stationary under a heavy fire and were fast expending their ammunition. The 37th continued slowly moving on without firing a shot; being paralysed with cold to such a degree that no persuasion of their officers could induce them to make any effort to dislodge the enemy, who took from some of them not only their firelocks but even the clothes from their persons.

Several men of the 44th supplied themselves with ammunition from the pouches of the Sipahees, and many proceeded to the front owing to their ammunition being expended. Major Scott and Captain Swinton, of the 44th, had also gone to the front severely wounded; and the command of the regiment devolved on Captain Souter.

Lieutenant Steer, of the 37th Native Infantry, with great difficulty succeeded in bringing to the rear a yaboo loaded with ammunition. But scarcely were the boxes placed on the ground, opened and a few rounds taken out than they were obliged to be abandoned; as, owing to our fire having slackened, the enemy became bolder and pressed upon the rear in great numbers. They had the advantage of being covered by our stragglers, which compelled our men to retire, firing volleys indiscriminately amongst them and the Afghans.

At this time our men were dropping fast from a flanking fire from the heights; and, seeing it was useless to attempt to maintain a position in the rear, under such circumstances, with only about 60 men, they were withdrawn; and with difficulty forced their way through the crowd to a more commanding position, where the rearguard of the 44th was joined by General Elphinstone, Colonel Chambers, of the 5th Light Cavalry, with some troopers, and Captain Hay, with a few of the Irregular Horse, and the only remaining gun, one having been abandoned in the pass. The 37th and the camp followers gradually passed to the front; but the Afghans were checked from following them.

After halting full an hour to let the stragglers get well to the front, they resumed their march; but, owing to the depth of the snow, the troops were compelled to assist the gun by manual labour, the horses being unable to get it on. In this way they reached the encamping ground without molestation from the enemy.

On leaving Cabool each Sipahee had 40 rounds of musket ammunition in pouch, with 100 spare loads. We have now not three camel loads left; and many Sipahees have not a single cartridge in pouch. Five hundred of our regular troops and about 2,500 of the camp followers are killed.

Poor Sturt was laid on the side of a bank, with his wife and myself beside him. It began snowing heavily: Johnson and Bygrave got some xummuls thrown over us. Dr Bryce, Horse Artillery, came and examined Sturt's wound. He dressed it; but I saw by the expression of his countenance that there was no hope. He afterwards kindly cut the ball out of my wrist and dressed both my wounds.

Half of a Sipahee's pall had been pitched, in which the ladies and their husbands took refuge. We had no one to scrape the snow off the ground in it. Captain Johnson and Mr Mein first assisted poor Sturt over to it, and then carried Mrs Sturt and myself through the deep snow. Mrs Sturt's bedding (saved by the ayah riding on it, whom we kept up close with ourselves) was now a comfort for my poor wounded son. He suffered dreadful agony all night, and intolerable thirst; and most grateful did we feel to Mr Mein for going out constantly to the stream to procure water. We had only a small vessel to fetch it in, which contained but a few mouthfuls. To sleep in such anxiety of mind and intense cold was impossible. There were nearly 30 of us packed together without room to turn.

The Sipahees and camp followers, half-frozen, tried to force their way not only into the tent, but actually into our beds, if such resting places can be so called – a posteen (or pelisse of sheepskin) half spread on the snow, and the other half wrapped over one.

Many poor wretches died round the tent in the night.

The light company of the 54th Native Infantry, which left Cabool 80 strong 36 hours previously, was reduced to 18 files. This is only one instance, which may fairly be taken as a general average of the destruction of our force.

Sunday, January 9, 1842

Before sunrise the same confusion as yesterday. Without any order given, or bugle sounded, three-fourths of our fighting men had pushed on in advance with the camp followers. As many as could had appropriated to themselves all the public yaboos and camels, on which they mounted.

A portion of the troops had also regularly moved off, the only order appearing to be, 'Come along; we are all going, and half the men are off, with the camp followers in advance!' We had gone perhaps a mile when the whole were remanded back to their former ground; and a halt for the day was ordered, in accordance with the wishes of the sirdar; who had represented to the general, through Captain Skinner, that his arrangements were not made as regarded either our security or provisions. Skinner urged the general to some mark of confidence in the sirdar's promises; which he instantly did by sending Captain Anderson to order back the troops and baggage.

Mrs Trevor kindly rode a pony, and gave up her place in the kajawa to Sturt, who must otherwise have been left to die on the ground. The rough motion increased his suffering and accelerated his death, but he was still conscious that his wife and I were with him; and we had the sorrowful satisfaction of giving him a Christian burial.

More than half of the force is now frost-bitten or wounded; and most of the men can scarcely put a foot to the ground.

This is the fourth day that our cattle have had no food; and the men are starved with cold and hunger.

Reports are prevalent in camp that the Irregular Cavalry and the envoy's escort are about to desert to Mahomed Akbar Khan; and also that the Afghans are tampering with our Sipahees to leave us and return to Cabool. The subahdar major of the 37th Native Infantry has deserted.

Shortly after Pottinger, Mackenzie and Lawrence arrived at the Khoord Cabool fort with the sirdar, he turned to Lawrence and said that he had a proposal to make, but that he did not like to do so lest his motives might be misconstrued; but that, as it concerned us more than himself, he would mention it; and that it was that all the married men, with their families, should come over and put themselves under his protection; he guaranteeing them honourable treatment and safe escort to Peshawur. He added that Lawrence must have seen from the events of the day previous – the loss of Captain Boyd's and Captain Anderson's children, etc. – that our camp was no place of safety for the ladies and children. Lawrence replied that he considered the proposition a most admirable one; and Skinner coming in just then, he repeated what had been passed to him. Skinner replied: 'This is just what I was thinking of suggesting.' On which Lawrence begged he would go off and get the general's sanction and bring them all without delay. Major Pottinger concurred entirely in the expediency of this measure.

Our present position is one of imminent peril. Immediately on Skinner's arrival about midday, we set off escorted by some chiefs to a fort about two miles distant, where Mahomed Akbar Khan had taken up his temporary residence. Captain Troup, brigade-major to the Shah's force, who was wounded, accompanied the party, as did also Mr Mein of the 13th, who, having been sent back with a year's sick leave to Cabool, after he was wounded in October, followed Mrs Sturt's and my fortunes, not being attached to any corps, nor having any duty to perform.

There can be little doubt but that the proposition was acceded to by the general in the twofold hope of placing the ladies and children beyond the dangers and dreadful privations of the camp, and also of showing the sirdar that he was sincere in his wish to negotiate a truce and thus win from him a similar feeling of confidence.

Overwhelmed with domestic affliction, neither Mrs Sturt nor I were in a fit state to decide for ourselves whether we would accept the sirdar's protection or not. There was but faint hope of our ever getting safe to Jellalabad, and we followed the stream. But although there was much talk regarding our going over, all I personally know of the affair is that I was told we were all to go, and that our horses were ready and we must mount immediately and be off.

We were taken by a very circuitous route to the Khoord Cabool forts, where we found Mahomed Akbar Khan and the hostages Mr Boyd's little boy had been brought there and was restored to his parents. Mrs Burnes and young Stoker were also saved and joined our party. Anderson's little girl is said to have been taken to Cabool, to the Nawab Zeman Shah Khan.

Three rooms were cleared out for us, having no outlets except a small door to each; and of course they were dark and dirty. The party to which I belonged consisted of Mrs Trevor and seven children, Lieutenant and Mrs Waller and child, Mrs Sturt, Mr Mein and myself, Mrs Smith and Mrs Burnes, two soldiers' wives and young Stoker, child of a soldier of the 13th, who was saved from people who were carrying him off to the hills and came in covered, we fear, with his mother's blood: of her we have no account, nor of Mrs Cunningham, both of the 13th. The dimensions of our room are at the utmost 14 feet by 10 feet.

At midnight some mutton bones and greasy rice were brought to us. All that Mrs Sturt and I possess are the clothes on our backs in which we quitted Cabool.

Here I must divide the account. I shall go on with my own personal adventures; and afterwards, from the same date, follow up the fortunes of our unhappy army, from the journals of friends who, thank God!, have lived through all their sufferings.

Monday, January 10, 1842

Mahomed Akbar Khan left us to escort our troops. Five hundred deserters are said to have come in to him. It is reported that the thieves have nearly exterminated our force, and that four of Mahomed Akbar's sirdars are killed. Akbar is expected back at night; and if the road is clear, we are to march at night and go 30 miles. Some officers are said to have taken refuge in a fort near this place. A letter came from the general, stating that he wished Captain Anderson and Captain Boyd to return: this was in consequence of a representation made to him that Anderson's making over the command of his corps to Lieutenant Le Geyt, and then going away, might have a bad effect on his men, who now showed symptoms of an inclination to leave us to our fate. But it was decided by the politicals that for those officers to return would have the appearance of their faith in the sirdar's promises being shaken, and that it would be productive of much evil: they remained therefore with us. Here was another instance of the general's vacillation. Anderson, on his return from taking the message to bring the troops back, was ordered by the general to go off with the other married men and families. Whatever may have been his own sentiments on the occasion, his opinion was never asked and he had but to obey.

Tuesday, January 11, 1842

We marched. We were necessitated to leave all the servants that could not walk; the sirdar promising that they should be fed. It would be impossible for me to describe the feelings with which we pursued our way through the dreadful scenes that awaited us. The road covered with awfully mangled bodies, all naked: 58 Europeans were counted in the Tunghee and the dip of the nullah; the natives innumerable. Numbers of camp followers, still alive, frost-bitten and starving; some perfectly out of their senses and idiotic. Major Ewart, 54th, and Major Scott, 44th, were recognized as we passed them; with some others. The sight was dreadful; the smell of the blood sickening; and the corpses lay so thick it was impossible to look from them, as it required care to guide my horse so as not to tread upon the bodies; but it is unnecessary to dwell on such a distressing and revolting subject.

We hear that Mahomed Akbar Khan offered to escort the army down, provided the troops laid down their arms; but that the general went on upon his own responsibility.

We arrived at the Tezeen fort, where we were well treated; and where we found Lieutenant Melville, 54th. He had, in guarding the colour of his regiment, received five severe wounds. He had fortunately seven rupees about him; these he gave to an Afghan to take him to the sirdar, who dressed his wounds with his own hands, applying burnt rags, and paid him every attention.

Wednesday, January 12, 1842

We went to Seh Baba; and thence out of the road, following the bed of the river, to Abdoollah Khan's fort. We passed our last gun, abandoned, with poor Dr Cardew's body lying on it, and three Europeans close by it.

During the march, we were joined by Mr Magrath, surgeon of the 37th Native Infantry, and six men of the 44th. He had been wounded and taken prisoner on the 10th whilst endeavouring to rally a party of some 40 or 50 Irregular Cavalry and bring them to the assistance of the unfortunate wounded men, who were being butchered at the bottom of the Huft Kotool. On his coming up with this party, and again ordering them to halt, to his great disgust he found Khoda Buksh Khan, a Ghilzie chief, amongst them; to whom they were apologizing for not having gone over the day previous, as their comrades had done. Mr Magrath had several narrow escapes; and, when surrounded by Ghilzie footmen with their long knives drawn, owed his life in a great measure to an Afghan horseman, who recognized him as having shown some little kindness to some of his sick friends at Cabool.

At night we had snow.

Our whole party, ladies and gentlemen, crammed into one room; one side of which was partitioned off with mats and filled with grain. Here an old woman cooked chupattis for us, three for a rupee; but finding the demand great, she soon raised the price to a rupee each.

Thursday, January 13, 1842

We travelled over mountain paths, where the camels found it difficult to get on with the kajawas, till we arrived at Jugduluk. Near the Ghavoy there had been fearful slaughter, principally of Europeans.

We found General Elphinstone, Brigadier Shelton and Captain Johnson here in tents.

Having brought our party safe to Jugduluk, I now return to the proceedings of our unfortunate army; taking up the tale when the ladies and their party took protection.

Sunday, January 9, 1842

A round Afghan tent was pitched for the ladies; and we felt the courtesy of the sirdars, who slept in the open air to give us shelter, even such as it was, for the wind blew in in every direction.

Immediately after our departure the Irregular Horse, with the exception of about 80 men, went over in a body to the sirdar; and as they were afterwards seen in company with a body of Afghan horse at about a mile distance, there was an attack from them apprehended: all was consternation. Several of our Sipahees absented themselves during the day, also a number of camp followers. A message was sent to Mahomed Akbar Khan, and a hope expressed that he would not favour the desertion of the troops; and he promised that all going over to him should be shot, which was immediately made known to the men. One of the mission chuprassies was caught in the act of going off, and he was shot.

Lieutenant Mackay, assistant to Captain Johnson, was sent in the afternoon to the sirdar (to the fort where the ladies were) for the purpose of being the bearer of a letter to General Sale at Jellalabad to order him to evacuate his position. This letter was written by Major Pottinger.

All the doolie bearers either deserted or were murdered the first day.

The whole of the camels and yaboos have been either taken by the enemy or plundered by our no less lawless camp followers and soldiers.

The greatest confusion prevailed all day; and anxiety and suspense for the ultimate fate of the army was intense; all expecting that if in a few hours they were not deprived of life by cold and hunger, they would fall by the knives of the Afghans; which, had they been then attacked, must indubitably have occurred, for on the return of the troops after their set-out in the morning, commanding officers had great difficulty in collecting 60 files a corps, but even of these many could scarcely hold a musket. Many died of cold and misery that night. To add to their wretchedness, many were nearly, and some wholly, afflicted with snow blindness.

Monday, January 10, 1842

No sooner was it light than the usual rush to the front was made by the mixed rabble of camp followers, Sipahees and Europeans in one huge mass. Hundreds of poor wretches, unable to seize any animals for themselves, or despoiled by stronger persons of those they had, were left on the road to die or be butchered.

After much exertion, the advance, consisting of the 44th, the only remaining 6-pounder and about 50 files of the 5th Cavalry, managed to get ahead of the crowd. The Afghans were appearing on the hills early: on arriving at the Tunghee Tareekee, a narrow gorge about 10 feet wide and two miles distant from their last ground, Captain Johnson was sent with the advance; the heights were taken possession of by the enemy; who fired down incessantly on the road, from which they were inaccessible. The snow increased in depth as the army advanced. There is a gradual ascent all the way from Khoord Cabool to Kubber-i-Jubhar, a distance of five miles; the progress was necessarily slow, and many poor fellows were shot. After getting through the pass, not above 50 yards in length, they proceeded to Kubber-i-Jubhar, where they halted for their comrades.

Latterly no Afghans had been seen, except at a distance; the horror of our people was therefore the greater when a few stragglers from the rear came up and reported themselves as the remnant of the rear column, almost every man of which had been either killed or wounded. Captain Hopkins had his arm broken by a musket ball. There was now not a single Sipahee left of the whole Cabool force.

A desperate attack had been made by a body of Afghans, sword in hand. Our men made no resistance; they threw away their arms and accoutrements and fell an easy prey to our barbarous and bloodthirsty foe.

The rearguard was composed of the 54th Regiment. On arriving at the narrow pass called Tunghee Tareekee, or the dark pass, a turn in the road shut out from their sight the enemy, who had followed close on their heels but on whom they had received strict orders not to fire; although the Ghilzies, from the heights and ravines, had kept up a sharp discharge, killing many Sipahees and camp followers and cutting up all wounded and sick left behind. On arriving at the above-mentioned pass, the turn in the road allowed the Ghilzies to close up, and a general attack was made on all sides. Hundreds of Afghans rushed down from the rocks and hills and cut to pieces their now reduced regiment. Here Major Ewart, commanding 54th, had both his arms broken by bullets from the jezails; Lieutenant Morrison, the adjutant, was wounded, and Lieutenant Weaver, of the same corps, slightly wounded.

Lieutenant Melville, on observing that the jemadar who carried the regiment's colour was wounded and dropping his charge, seized it; and, after vainly attempting to tear it off the staff, to which it was too firmly attached, made his way on foot (his horse having been killed) with the colour in his hand. This made him a mark for the enemy; and ere he had got out of the pass, being nearly, or quite, the last man of the column, or rather rabble, he received a spear wound in his back, which threw him on his face. Ere well able to rise, a severe sword-cut in the head again laid him prostrate but he contrived to crawl as far as the fast retreating column; then the knife of an Afghan wounding him in the neck, and a spear in the chin, he gave up all for lost.

He was now surrounded by a dozen Ghilzies; and no man, save the dead and dying, near him. Then the enemy, observing a box of treasure on the opposite side of the pass, left him for the purpose of rifling the money, either supposing they had already killed him or intending to return when they had secured the more valuable booty. This pause gave Lieutenant Melville an opportunity of escaping and regaining the column, which, although weak from his wounds, he availed himself of. By going through the snow in the ravines he contrived to reach the column, where a pony without an owner, or saddle of any description, presenting itself, he scrambled on to it, and gained the centre of the column, where the 44th and one gun still kept some order. Lieutenant Melville was tied on the gun and was told by General Elphinstone that he should be sent over to the charge of the sirdar, Mahomed Akbar Khan, on reaching Tezeen, or at any opportunity of going.

On a report of a large body of horse being observed in the rear, the gun was ordered there; and Lieutenant Melville was placed on a bank on the roadside. The column passed on; and he was expecting the fate of the other poor fellows who had fallen when, providentially for him, a horseman who had known him in cantonments rode up, strapped him on his horse and took him over to the party of horsemen, consisting of Mahomed Akbar Khan and his followers. They received him most kindly and, binding up his wounds, gave him a loonghee, his regimental cap being cut to pieces. (The loonghee is the cloth commonly worn as a turban by the Afghans, and it is generally of blue check with a red border: those worn by the Khyberrees are much gayer and have a large admixture of yellow.) Melville gave to Omer Khan, the horseman who saved his life, seven rupees, being all the property he possessed.

Every particle of baggage was gone.

The small remnant of the army consisted of about 70 files of the 44th, 50 of the 5th Cavalry and one 6-pounder gun. Observing a body of cavalry in their rear, they determined to bring their solitary gun into position and make a last effort for existence. Finding it was again Mahomed Akbar Khan, Captain Skinner, by direction of the general, went over to him under escort to remonstrate on the attack made on our troops after a treaty had been entered into for our protection. He replied that he regretted it;

he could not control the Ghilzies (the inhabitants of this part of the country) with his small body of horse, about 300; but, as the remnant of our troops was merely a few Europeans, he would guarantee their safety, and that of all the European officers, to Jellalabad if the general would conduct them all disarmed, although the Afghans were to have the use of their weapons. He said his motives for this were that, should they bring their arms with them, his own followers would be afraid of treachery. To this proposition the general would not assent. Mackay returned with Skinner from the sirdar, as the road to Jellalabad was said to be unsafe.

The troops continued their fearful march; the remnant of the camp followers, with several wounded officers, went ahead. For five miles they saw no enemy. All who could not walk were necessarily left behind. They descended a long steep descent to the bed of the Tezeen nullah. At this dip the scene was horrible: the ground was covered with dead and dying, amongst whom were several officers. They had been suddenly attacked and overpowered. The enemy here crowded from the tops of the hills in all directions down the bed of the nullah, through which the route lay for three miles; and our men continued their progress through an incessant fire from the heights on both sides until their arrival in the Tezeen valley, at about half-past four in the afternoon. The descent from the Huft Kotool was about 2,000 feet; and here they lost the snow.

About 12,000 persons have perished!

A quarter of an hour after their arrival, the sirdar and a party came into the valley to a fort higher up belonging to his father-in-law, Mahomed Shah Khan. A signal was made to his horsemen to approach: two came, and Captain Skinner, by the general's desire, accompanied them to Mahomed Akbar Khan to devise some means of saving the remnant – about 4,000 people of all descriptions. Skinner returned at dusk and brought back the same message as from Kubber-i-Jubhar regarding disarming the Europeans; again this was refused.

The general then decided, weak and famished as the troops were, and without any prospect of procuring provisions at Tezeen, to march at seven in the evening (they had left Khoord Cabool, 15 miles from Tezeen, at half-past six in the morning) and proceed, if possible, through the Jugduluk Pass by eight or nine the next morning. In this consisted their only chance of safety; for, should the enemy obtain intimation of their approach, the pass would be occupied and the object defeated. Johnson pointed out to the general that Mahomed Akbar Khan and his party could, by means of a short cut across the mountains, start long after them and arrive before them, ready to oppose them. Jugduluk is about 24 miles from Tezeen; the pass is about two miles long, very narrow and commanded on both sides by high and precipitous hills.

At Tezeen General Elphinstone received a note in cipher from Captain Conolly, warning him that Mahomed Akbar Khan had quitted Cabool with the avowed intention of getting into his hands the person of the general and all the married people with their families.

A message was sent to Mahomed Akbar Khan that they were going to march to Seh Baba, seven miles from Tezeen (this place is sometimes called Tukeea-i-Fakeer). The road lies down the bed of a nullah, with high hills on either side. The place is only remarkable for having a few trees and a grave or two under them; and from the latter I believe it takes its name.

The camp followers having been the bane of this unfortunate army, they hoped to move off quietly and leave them behind; but no sooner did they start than they found that all who were able to stand were accompanying them. They left their remaining gun; and Dr Cardew, who was mortally wounded at the dip into the Tezeen nullah, was laid on the carriage to await death, which was rapidly approaching. He was found dead by Mahomed Akbar's people the next morning.

The night was fine and moonlit, and they reached Seh Baba about midnight; here a few shots were fired on them; and the rear being attacked, the whole remains of the 44th, with the exception of about nine files to form the advance, were ordered there. Thus the column remained until their arrival at Jugduluk, their progress being again impeded by that evil which always attends Indian armies – the camp followers, who, if a shot is fired in advance, invariably fall back; and if the shot is in the rear, rush to the front.

Tuesday, January 11, 1842

From Seh Baba the road turns off sharp to the right over the mountains to Jugduluk; across the nullah is seen the short road to Cabool, which cannot be travelled by guns or camels.

At Seh Baba, Dr Duff (the surgeon-general to the forces in Afghanistan), who had had his hand cut off with a penknife at Tezeen, in consequence of a severe wound, was from weakness obliged to lag behind and was two days afterwards found murdered.

Bareekub is three miles from Seh Baba: there is a clear stream of water, and several caves cut in the rocks. Here our force observed a number of people in the caves, with whom they did not interfere, as they did not molest them. They eventually fired some volleys on the rear.

At daybreak the advance arrived at Killa Sung, about seven miles from Seh Baba, where there are some streams of water: this is the general encamping ground, though very confined, and is commanded by hills all round.

They proceeded about half a mile further on and then halted, until the rearguard should arrive; but they, having been much molested on the road, did not arrive for two hours. On their first arrival not an Afghan was to be seen; but shortly several made their appearance on the hills, and the number continued every moment to increase. Not a drop of water was procurable; nor would they get any until their arrival at Jugduluk. They had marched for 24 hours consecutively, and had still 10 miles to go before they could hope for rest. On being joined by the rearguard they continued their march, the enemy in small numbers watching every opportunity to murder stragglers from the column.

At two miles from Jugduluk the descent into the valley commences. The hills on each side of the road were occupied by the enemy, who kept firing from their long jezails; and again the road was covered with dead and dying, as they were in such a mass that every shot told.

On arrival in the valley, a position was taken up on the first height near some ruined walls. As scarcely any Europeans of the advance now remained, and the enemy were increasing, the general called all the officers (about 20) to form line and show a front: they had scarcely done so when Captain Grant, Assistant Adjutant-General, received a ball through the cheek which broke his jaw.

On the arrival of the rearguard, followed up by the enemy, the latter took possession of two heights close to our position: on which our force went for security within the ruined walls. The men were almost maddened with hunger and thirst; a stream of pure water ran within 150 yards of the position, but no man could go for it without being massacred.

For about half an hour they had a respite from the fire of the enemy, who now only watched their proceedings.

The general desired Johnson to see if there were any bullocks or camels procurable amongst the followers: he obtained three bullocks, which were killed, served out and – although raw – devoured instantly by the Europeans.

A few horsemen coming in sight, they signed for one to approach: he did so, and on being questioned what chief was present, said Mahomed Akbar Khan. A message was sent to the sirdar by the general to know why they were again molested. The chief replied that he wished to converse with Skinner, who immediately accompanied the messenger. This was about half past three in the afternoon of the 11th.

After marching for 30 hours they lay down on the ground, worn out by cold, hunger, thirst and fatigue: but scarcely had Skinner taken his departure, when volley after volley was poured into the enclosure where they were resting. All was instant confusion, and a general rush took place outside the walls; men and cattle all huddled together, each striving to hide himself from the murderous fire of the enemy.

At this time 20 gallant men of the 44th made a simultaneous rush down the hill to drive the enemy off the heights they occupied; in this they were successful, for, supposing they were followed by the rest, the foe took to flight ere our men could reach their position.

In about a quarter of an hour, as so small a party would not admit of any division, this party was recalled. They again entered within the broken walls; and instantly our inveterate foes were in their former position dealing death amongst them.

About five o'clock Skinner returned with a message that the sirdar wished to see the general, Brigadier Shelton and Johnson; and if they would go over to confer with him, he would engage to put a stop to any further massacre, give food to our troops and, on condition of their remaining with him as hostages for General Sale's evacuation of Jellalabad, escort all the small remaining party in safety.

Mahomed Shah Khan, father-in-law to the sirdar, and whose daughter is with the Dost at Loodiana, is one of the principal Ghilzie chiefs. He came at dusk with an escort to receive them; and they started in the confident hope that some arrangement would be entered into to save the lives of the remainder of the army. The general and the above-mentioned officers proceeded to the top of the valley for about two miles and found the sirdar and his party in bivouac.

Nothing could exceed the kind manner in which they were received. The chief, on hearing they had not tasted food for 48 hours, had a cloth spread on the ground and a good pillau and other dishes, as also tea, were quickly brought forth. They formed a circle round it, and all ate out of the same dish. Their hunger, though great, was not to be compared to their thirst, which had not been quenched for two days.

The party consisted of the sirdar, Mahomed Akbar Khan, Mahomed Shah Khan, Abdool Ghyas Khan (son of Jubbar Khan) and a young lad called Abdool Hakeem Khan, nephew to the sirdar. The attention of the sirdar and his party was excessive; and after dinner they sat round a blazing fire and conversed on various subjects. The general requested that Mahomed Akbar Khan would early in the morning forward provisions to the troops and make arrangements for supplying them with water – all of which he faithfully promised to do.

The general was anxious for permission to return to his troops; and offered to send Brigadier Anquetil should the sirdar require an officer in his stead. Johnson, by the general's desire, pointed out to the sirdar the stigma that would attach to him as commander of the force if he were to remain in a place of comparative security whilst such danger impended over the troops. To this the sirdar would not consent. At about 11 p.m. the sirdar promised he would early in the morning call the chiefs of the pass together to make arrangements for a safe escort. He then showed them into a small tent where, stretched on their cloaks, they found relief in sleep.

Our unfortunate force at Jugduluk this day consisted of 150 men of the 44th, 16 dismounted horse artillery men and 25 of the 5th Cavalry; not a single Sipahee with arms and no spare ammunition; the few rounds in pouch had been taken from the killed.

Wednesday, January 12, 1842

The English officers arose at sunrise, and found the sirdar and his party were up. They showed them the same civility as overnight: two confidential servants of the chief were appointed to wait on them, and they were warned not to attempt to leave the tent without one of these men, lest they should be maltreated or insulted by the Ghilzies, who were flocking in to pay their respects to Mahomed Akbar.

About 9 a.m. the chiefs of the pass and the country around Sookhab arrived. Sookhab is about 13 miles from Jugduluk, towards Jellalabad, and is the usual halting ground.

The chiefs sat down to discuss affairs. They were bitter in their hatred towards us, and declared that nothing would satisfy them and their men but our extermination. Money they would not receive. The sirdar, as far as words could prove his sincerity, did all in his power to conciliate them; and, when all other arguments failed, reminded them that his father and family were in the power of the British government at Loodiana; and that vengeance would be taken on the latter if mercy were not showed to the British in their power.

Mahomed Shah Khan offered them 60,000 rupees on condition of our force not being molested. After some time they took their departure to consult with their followers. Mahomed Shah Khan mentioned to Johnson that he feared the chiefs would not, without some great inducement, resist the temptation of plunder and murder that now offered itself; he wound up the discourse by asking if we would give them two lacs of rupees for a free passage. On this being explained to the general, he gave his consent; this was made known to Mahomed Shah Khan, who went away and promised to return quickly.

The general again begged of the sirdar to permit him to return to his troops; but without avail.

Johnson, by the general's desire, wrote early in the day to Skinner, to come to the sirdar. This letter and two others, it is to be feared, he never received. A report was brought in that Skinner was wounded, but not dangerously. The sirdar expressed much sorrow; poor Skinner died of his wound the same day.

Until twelve o'clock crowds of Ghilzies, with their respective chiefs, continued to pour in from the surrounding country to make their salaams to Mahomed Akbar Khan, to participate in the plunder of our unfortunate people and to revel in the massacre of the Europeans. From their expressions of hatred towards our whole race, they appeared to anticipate more delight in cutting our throats than in the expected booty. However, on a hint from the sirdar, they changed the language in which they conversed from Persian to Pushtoo, which was not understood by our officers.

The sirdar, to all appearance, whilst sitting with Johnson, endeavoured to conciliate them; but it very probably was only done as a blind to hide his real feelings.

In two instances, the reply of the chiefs was: 'When Burnes came into this country, was not your father entreated by us to kill him; or he would go back to Hindoostan, and at some future day bring an army and take our country from us? He would not listen to our advice, and what is the consequence? Let us now, that we have the opportunity, take advantage of it; and kill those infidel dogs.'

At about twelve o'clock the sirdar left them and went on the top of a hill in rear of the British bivouac. He did not return till sunset; and in reply to the anxious inquiry when Mahomed Shah Khan would return, they were always told immediately. Frequent assurances had been given that the troops had been supplied with food and water; but subsequently they learnt that neither had been given them in their dire necessity.

The sirdar returned at dusk; and was soon followed by Mahomed Shah Khan, who brought intelligence that all was finally and amicably arranged for the safe conduct of the troops to Jellalabad. The sirdar said he would accompany them in the morning early. By the general's request, Johnson wrote to Brigadier Anquetil to have the troops in readiness to march by eight o'clock. He had also commenced a letter to General Sale to evacuate Jellalabad (this being part of the terms). Suddenly, and before the first note was sent off, much musketry was heard down the valley in the direction of the troops; and a report was brought in that the Europeans were moving off through the pass followed by the Ghilzies.

All was consternation. At first the sirdar suggested that he and the officers should follow them; in this the general concurred. In a few minutes the sirdar changed his mind; said he feared their doing so would injure the troops by bringing after them the whole horde of Ghilzies then assembled in the valley. He promised to send a confidential servant to Meer Ufzul Khan at Gundamuck (two miles beyond Sookhab) to afford them protection; and agreed to start with them at midnight, as being mounted they would overtake the others before daybreak. When about to separate for the night, the sirdar again altered the time of departure to the first hour of daylight. Remonstrances were of no avail; our party were too completely in the power of the enemy to persist in what they had not the power to enforce.

Mahomed Akbar Khan told Johnson, after Mahomed Shah Khan went out to consult with the chiefs of the pass, that the latter were dogs and no faith could be placed in them; he begged Johnson would send for three or four of his most intimate friends that their lives might be saved in the event of treachery to the troops. Gladly as he would have saved his individual friends, he was under the necessity of explaining to the sirdar that a sense of honour would prevent the officers deserting their men at a time of such imminent peril.

The sirdar also proposed that, in the event of the Ghilzies not acceding to the terms, he would himself, at dusk, proceed with a party of horsemen to the foot of the hill where our troops were, and, previous orders being sent to the commanding officer for all to be ready, he would bring every European away in safety by means of each of his horsemen taking up one behind him. The Ghilzies would not then fire upon them, lest they should hit him or his men. But he would not allow a single Hindoostanee to follow; as he could not protect 2,000 men (the computed number).

Johnson interpreted all this to the general, but it was deemed impracticable; from past experience they knew how impossible it was even to separate the Sipahees from the camp followers. Four or five times during the day they heard the report of musketry in the direction of our troops; but they were always told that all fighting had ceased. This was subsequently proved to be a gross falsehood. Our troops were incessantly fired upon from the time that the general and the other officers quitted them to the time of their departure, and several hundreds of officers and men had been killed or wounded. The remainder, maddened with cold, hunger and thirst, the communication between them and the general cut off, and seeing no prospect but certain death before them by remaining in their present position, determined on making one desperate effort to leave Jugduluk. Snow fell during the night.

My narrative now continues from information furnished by a friend remaining with the remnant of this ill-fated army. They halted this day at Jugduluk, hoping to negotiate an arrangement with Mahomed Akbar Khan and the Ghilzie chiefs, as before stated. But the continual firing, and frequent attempts made by the enemy to force them from their position during the day, but too well indicated that there was little or no chance of negotiations being effectual to quell hostilities and admit of their resuming their march in safety. On the contrary, there appeared an evident determination to harass their retreat to the very last.

Near the close of the day the enemy commenced a furious attack from all sides. The situation of our troops at this time was critical in the extreme: the loss they sustained in men and officers had been great during the day, and the survivors had only been able to obtain a scanty meal of camel's flesh. Even water was not procurable without the parties proceeding for it being exposed to a heavy fire. The men, under all this suffering and perishing with cold at their post, bravely repelled the enemy and would then have followed them from under the dilapidated walls had they been permitted to do so. During this conflict Captain Souter of the 44th, anxious to save the colours of his regiment, tore one of them from its staff and, folding it round his person, concealed it under the posteen he wore. The other was in like manner appropriated by Lieutenant Cumberland; but finding that he could not close his pea-coat over it, he reluctantly entrusted it to the care of the acting quartermaster-sergeant of the 44th Regiment.

Great anxiety prevailed amongst the troops, caused by the continued absence of General Elphinstone and Brigadier Shelton, the two seniors in command. As they did not return, it was resolved to resume the march as soon as the night should shroud them from observation, and Brigadier Anquetil, now in command, ordered the troops to fall in at eight o'clock. But before the men could take the places assigned to them, the camp followers, who were still numerous, crowded upon them as usual. At length between eight and nine o'clock they took their departure – a very trying scene due to the entreaties of the wounded, amounting to 70 or 80, for whom there was no conveyance. However heartrending to all, they were necessarily abandoned, with the painful conviction that they would be massacred in cold blood, defenceless as they were, by the first party of Ghilzies that arrived.

The enemy, who seem to have been aware of the intended removal, soon commenced an attack upon the straggling camp followers. A number of Afghans, favoured by the darkness of the night, stole in amongst the followers that were in column, quietly dispatched them and proceeded to plunder. These daring men, however, were nearly all cut up or bayoneted by the enraged soldiery who shortly after came upon an encampment of the enemy; in the passing they were saluted with a heavy fire, followed up by a sally upon the camp followers, as usual.

They proceeded on until they came to a gorge, with low steep hills on either side, between which the road passed, about two miles from Jugduluk. Here two barriers had been thrown across the road, constructed of bushes and branches of trees. The road, which had been flooded, was a mass of ice and the snow on the hills was very deep. The enemy, who had waited for them in great force at this spot, rushed upon the column, knife in hand. The camp followers and wounded men fell back upon the handful of troops for protection, thus rendering them powerless and causing the greatest confusion; whilst the men, in small detached parties, were maintaining conflicts with fearful odds against them.

In this conflict the acting quartermaster-sergeant fell. In the confusion caused by an overwhelming enemy pressing on the rear in a night attack, it is not surprising that it was found impossible to extricate the colour from the body of the fallen man, and its loss was unavoidable. The disorder of the troops was increased by a part of them, the few remaining horsemen, galloping through and over the infantry in hopes of securing their own retreat to Jellalabad. The men, maddened at being ridden over, fired on them; it is said that some officers were fired at; but that rests on doubtful testimony. When the firing slackened, and the clashing of knives and bayonets had in some measure ceased, the men moved on slowly, and on arriving at the top of the gorge were able to ascertain the fearful extent of the loss they had sustained in men and officers. Of the latter, Brigadier Anquetil and above 20 others were missing. The troops now halted unmolested for an hour, during which time a few stragglers contrived to join them.

The country being now of a more open description, our small force suffered less annoyance from the fire of the enemy, but the determination of the men to bring on their wounded comrades greatly retarded their marching; thus their pace did not exceed two miles in the hour. From time to time sudden attacks were made on the rear; particularly in spots where the road wound close under the foot of the hills, and there a sharp fire was sure to be met with. In this manner they went on till they reached the Sookhab River, which they forded below the bridge at 1 a.m. on the 13th, being aware that the enemy would take possession of it and dispute the passage. Whilst fording the river a galling fire was kept up from the bridge; here Lieutenant Cadett of the 44th and several men were killed and wounded.

Thursday, January 13, 1842

From Sookhab the remnant of the column moved towards Gundamuck. As the day dawned the enemy's numbers increased, and unfortunately daylight soon exposed to them how very few fighting men the column contained. The force now consisted of 20 officers, of whom Major Griffiths was the senior; 50 men of the 44th, six of the Horse Artillery and four or five Sipahees. Amongst the whole there were but 20 muskets. Three hundred camp followers still continued with them.

Being now assailed by an increased force, they were compelled to quit the road and take up a position on a hill adjoining. Some Afghan horsemen being observed at a short distance were beckoned to. On their approach there was a cessation of firing; terms were proposed by Captain Hay to allow the force to proceed to Jellalabad without further hostilities. These persons not being sufficiently influential to negotiate, Major Griffiths proceeded with them to a neighbouring chief for that purpose; taking with him Mr Blewitt, who was formerly a writer in Captain Johnson's office and who understood Persian, that he might act as interpreter.

Many Afghans ascended the hill where our troops awaited the issue of the expected conference, and exchanges of friendly words passed between both parties. This lasted upwards of an hour; but hostilities were renewed by the Afghans, who snatched at the firearms of the men and officers. This they of course resisted, and they drove them off the hill; but the majority of the enemy, who occupied the adjoining hills commanding our position, commenced a galling fire upon us.

Several times they attempted to dislodge our men from the hill and were repulsed until, our ammunition being expended and our fighting men reduced to about 30, the enemy made a rush, which in our weak state we were unable to cope with. They bore our men down knife in hand; and slaughtered all the party except Captain Souter and seven or eight men of the 44th and artillery. This officer thinks that this unusual act of forbearance towards him originated in the strange dress he wore: his posteen having opened during the last struggle exposed to view the colour he had wrapped round his body; and they probably thought they had secured a valuable prize in some great bahadur, for whom a large ransom might be obtained.

Eighteen officers and about 50 men were killed at the final struggle at Gundamuck.

From Lieutenant Eyre's Diary

It only remains to relate the fate of those few officers and men who rode on ahead of the rest after passing the barriers. Six of the 12 officers – Captains Bellow, Collier and Hopkins, Lieutenant Bird, Doctors Harpur and Brydon – reached Futteabad in safety, the other six having dropped gradually off by the way and been destroyed. Deceived by the friendly professions of some peasants near the above-named town, who brought them bread to eat, they unwisely delayed a few moments to satisfy the cravings of hunger. The inhabitants meanwhile armed themselves and, suddenly sallying forth, cut down Captain Bellow and Lieutenant Bird. Captains Collyer and Hopkins and Doctors Harpur and Brydon rode off and were pursued. The three former were overtaken and slain within four miles of Jellalabad; Dr Brydon, by miracle, escaped and was the only officer of the whole Cabool force who reached that garrison in safety.

Such was the memorable retreat of the British army from Cabool. Viewed in all its circumstances – and in the military conduct which preceded and brought about such a consummation, and the treachery, disaster and suffering which accompanied it – it is perhaps without parallel in all history.

As Lady Sale has described, a number of small groups of prisoners and hostages had been taken during the preceding weeks. The main party were taken under the command of Mahomed Akbar Khan and moved from one uncomfortable location to the next. They included the wives of the most senior officers, particularly Lady Macnaghten and Lady Sale, and also Lieutenant Eyre. Several attempts were made to persuade General Sale to release this group, which included his daughter as well as his wife, in exchange for his retirement from Jellalabad. All were resolutely refused.

It was not until September of the same year (1842) that British reinforcements arrived: two massive armies, one at Jellalabad and one at Candahar, both destined to move on Cabool. Only at this point did the Afghans negotiate and return the weary group of wives, with several small children, to the custody of Sir Robert Sale.

From Lady Sale's Diary

September 17, 1842

We had proceeded but a short way on our journey when a horseman arrived with a note informing us that Sale was close at hand with a brigade. I had had fever hanging about me for some days; and, being scarce able to sit on my horse, had taken my place in a kajawa, the horrid motion of which had made me feel ten times worse than before I entered it. But this news renovated my strength. I shook off fever and all ills and anxiously awaited his arrival, of which a cloud of dust was the forerunner. General Nott was near Urghundee, and consequently close to us, and General Pollock requested he would send a brigade to our assistance. This he refused, much to the disgust of his officers, alleging that his troops were fatigued. On this General Pollock sent Sale with a brigade, at a few hours' notice. He left Siah Sung two miles east of Cabool; and made a forced march on the 19th (his 60th birthday) to Urghundee. He halted there that night, and on the following morning left his camp standing and marched to meet us. At the pass near Kote Ashruffee he left his infantry to hold the position and proceeded at the head of the 3rd Dragoons. A party of Sultan Jan's men were in this neighbourhood; and some Kokhees in the immediate vicinity were driven off by the jezailchees. Had we not received assistance, our recapture was certain, but, as it was, they dared not attack the force they saw.

It is impossible to express our feelings on Sale's approach. To my daughter and myself happiness, so long delayed as to be almost unexpected, was actually painful, and accompanied by a choking sensation, which could not obtain the relief of tears. When we arrived where the infantry were posted, they cheered all the captives as they passed them. They also, most considerately, informed me of Sale having been struck by a spent ball without injury, and congratulated me on our gracious queen's bestowal of the highest order of the Bath upon my gallant husband – a distinction, I believe, unparalleled in his present rank and therefore the more dearly prized.

During this march, many curiously formed rocks were seen at a distance, one bearing a strong resemblance to a giant climbing up the precipice; another so perfect when near as to render one doubtful whether the bull couchant was not the remains of ancient Hindoo sculpture. We did not fail to drink of the mineral spring as we passed it; and whilst so employed, attracted the attention of a party of Afghans, to whom Major Pottinger recommended a hearty draught of this sparkling liquid, which, however pleasing to the eye, is far from being so to the palate, being very like ink. The grave Afghans drank a full cup of it, exclaiming, 'Shookr!' and 'Joor Ustie!' – 'Praise be to God!' and 'That we may grow strong on it!' They then stroked down their beards and wended their way with great satisfaction. The latter part of our road lay along a narrow path, on either side of a tributary stream, bounded by a high and precipitous range of slate-stone rocks. We soon came to the Helmund, which we crossed, and encamped on its bank. Nearly opposite to us, a part of the rocks presented the form of a seated figure of Boodha.

September 19, 1842

We marched two hours before daylight, and crossed the Onai Kotui, a succession of ascents and descents, and some of them very steep, ending in a defile; after which the road was very stony. The grain was still green in many parts; but some of it was not only cut but also carried away. We passed Killa Onai, Killa Suffard, and Killa Mustapha Khan. At the latter, breakfast was prepared; nan (native sweet cakes) and tea for all who chose to partake of it en passant. The proprietor of this fort, a friend, pressed forward to welcome us individually. Most of the men had a little word of hearty congratulation to offer, each in his own style, on the restoration of his colonel's wife and daughter. My highly wrought feelings found the desired relief and, while the long withheld tears now found their course, I could scarcely speak to thank the soldiers for their sympathy.

On arriving at the camp, Captain Backhouse fired a royal salute from his Mountain Train guns, and not only our old friends, but all the officers in the party, came to offer congratulations and welcome our return from captivity.

From Lieutenant Eyre's Diary

September 20, 1842

All doubt was now at an end; we were once more under the safeguard of British troops. General Sale was there in person, and his happiness at regaining his long-lost wife and daughter can be imagined. The gallant veteran's countenance was an index of his feelings, and apathetic indeed must have been the heart that failed to sympathize with his holy joy. Fervent were our aspirations of praise to Heaven at this happy, and of late unlooked for, termination of all our hardships and anxieties. Surely never has the hand of Providence been more clearly discernible than in the wonderful preservation of so many ladies and children, through scenes of a nature to quail the stoutest heart and injure the strongest constitution; but more particularly in restraining the wrath of savage men, whose intense hatred of us was only equalled by their unscrupulous cruelty, and who longed to wreak their revenge upon us for the wrongs, whether real or fancied, that they had suffered at the hands of our nation.

Our friends in camp at Urghundee received us with overflowing kindness, and we soon found ourselves in circumstances far more favourable than we had known for nine tedious months of suffering and sorrow.

From Lady Sale's Diary

September 20, 1842

We marched to Killa Kazee, and great was the contrast of our present happiness and comfort compared with what our state had been when we last bivouacked under the trees at this place. The obnoxious fort was deserted; but the troops obtained forage there. The place was destroyed by fire, as was also a fort of Sultan Jan's. But guards were sent to the Kuzzilbash forts near us to protect the property of our friends. A reward has been offered for Captain Bygrave, and it is supposed he will be brought in to us shortly. At three o'clock we resumed our march to Cabool and passed through the great bazaar. The shops were shut and all looked very desolate – unlike the busy city it was when we were here last year and the inhabitants found their trade prosper under our rule. We were greeted, on our arrival at the camp at Siah Sung, with a salute of 21 guns.

And now my notes may end. Any further journals of mine can only be interesting to those nearly connected to me.

Major-General Pollock to Major-General Lumley

Camp, Cabool, September 22, 1842

Being apprehensive that attempts would be made to intercept the prisoners, I detached Major-General Sir R. Sale with troops, on the 19th instant, to the Urghundee Pass; and the circumstances proved fortunate, as a delay of 24 hours would have enabled Sultan Jan, who was in pursuit, to overtake our people. I am happy to state that the whole who were in confinement – with the exception of Captain Bygrave, who is with Mahomed Akbar – arrived in my camp yesterday evening.

GEORGE POLLOCK

List of prisoners released on September 21, 1842

Major-General Shelton, Her Majesty's 44th Foot
Lieutenant-Colonel Palmer, 27th Bengal Native Infantry
Major Griffiths, 37th Bengal Native Infantry
Captain Boyd, Commissariat
Captain Johnson, Commissariat, 26th Native Infantry
Captain Burnett, 14th Native Infantry
Captain Souter, Her Majesty's 44th Foot
Captain Waller, Bengal Horse Artillery
Captain Alston, 27th Native Infantry
Captain Poett, 27th Native Infantry
Captain Walsh, 52nd Madras Native Infantry
Captain Drummond, 3rd Bengal Light Cavalry
Lieutenant Eyre, Bengal Artillery
Lieutenant Airey, Her Majesty's 3rd Buffs
Lieutenant Warburton, Bengal Artillery
Lieutenant Webb, 38th Madras Native Infantry
Lieutenant Crawford, Bengal 3rd Native Infantry
Lieutenant Mein, Her Majesty's 13th Light Infantry
Lieutenant Harris, 27th Bengal Native Infantry
Lieutenant Melville, 54th Bengal Native Infantry
Lieutenant Evans, Her Majesty's 44th Foot
Ensign Haughton, 31st Bengal Native Infantry
Ensign Williams, 27th Bengal Native Infantry
Ensign Nicholson, 27th Bengal Native Infantry

Conductor Ryley, Ordnance Commissariat
Surgeon McGrath
Assistant Surgeons Berwick and Thomson

Lady Macnaghten
Lady Sale
Mrs Sturt and one child
Mrs Mainwaring and one child
Mrs Boyd and three children
Mrs Eyre and one child
Mrs Waller and two children
Mrs Ryley, wife of Conductor Ryley, and three children
Mrs Bourne, wife of Private Bourne, 13th Light Infantry
Mrs Wade, wife of Sergeant Wade

Major Pottinger, Bombay Artillery
Captain Lawrence, 11th Light Cavalry
Captain Mackenzie, 48th Madras Native Infantry

Mr Fallon and Mr Blewitt, clerks, not in the service

Her Majesty's 44th Foot Sergeants Wedlock, Weir and Fair; Corporals Sumpter and Bevan; Drummers Higgins, Lovell and Branagan; Privates Burns, Cresham, Cronin, Driscoll, Deroney, Duffy, Mathews, McDade, Marron, McCarthey, McCabe, Nowlan, Robson, Seyburne, Shean, Tongue, Wilson, Durant, Arch, Stott, Moore, Millar, Murphy, Marshall, Cox, Robinson, Brady and McGlynn; Boys, Grier and Milwood

Her Majesty's 13th Light Infantry Privates Binding, Murray, Magary, Monks, Maccullar, McConnell and Cuff

Bengal Horse Artillery Sergeants Cleland and McNee; Gunners Dulton, Hearn and Keane; Sergeant Wade, baggage sergeant to the Cabool Mission

G. PONSONBY

Lieutenant Eyre recorded in his diary a visit made by himself and Lady Sale, during their captivity, to see the famous Buddhist figures in the rock at Bamian.

Tim Coates Books

Crime
The Great British Train Robbery, 1963 (Illustrated)
Rillington Place, 1949
The Strange Story of Adolf Beck
The Trials of Oscar Wilde, 1895

Ireland
Bloody Sunday: Lord Widgery's report, 1972
The Irish Book of Death and Flying Ships (Illustrated)
The Irish Uprising, 1914–21
The Theft of the Irish Crown Jewels: the unsolved mystery (Illustrated, forthcoming)

Transport
The Loss of the Titanic, 1912
R.101: the airship disaster, 1930
Tragic Journeys (Titanic, R.101, Munich Air Crash)

Travel and British Empire
The Amritsar Massacre: General Dyer in the Punjab, 1919
The Boer War: Ladysmith and Mafeking, 1900
The British Invasion of Tibet: Colonel Younghusband, 1904
The British War in Afghanistan: the dreadful retreat from Kabul in 1842 (Illustrated)
Florence Nightingale and the Crimea, 1854–55
King Guezo of Dahomey, 1850–52
Mr Hosie's Journey to Tibet, 1904
Peace in Tibet: the Younghusband expedition, 1904 (Illustrated, forthcoming)
The Siege Collection (Kars, Boer War, Peking)
The Siege of Kars, 1855
The Siege of the Peking Embassy, 1900
Travels in Mongolia, 1902
Wilfrid Blunt's Egyptian Garden: fox–hunting in Cairo

Tudor history
Letters of Henry VIII, 1526–29

UK politics since 1945
The Hutton Inquiry, 2003
John Profumo and Christine Keeler, 1963
Lord Butler's Report: Espionage and the Iraq War
The Scandal of Christine Keeler and John Profumo: Lord Denning's report (Illustrated)

'Spitting Tacks': Lord Fraser's Report into the building of the Scottish Parliament
UFOs in the House of Lords, 1979
War in the Falklands, 1982

United States of America
The Assassination of John F. Kennedy, 1963
The Cuban Missile Crisis, 1962
John Lennon: the FBI files (Illustrated)
Marilyn Monroe: the FBI files (Illustrated)
Nixon and Watergate: the Watergate Special Prosecution report (Illustrated, forthcoming)
Sacco and Vanzetti: the FBI files (Illustrated, forthcoming)
The St Valentine's Day Massacre, 1929
The Shooting of John F. Kennedy, 1963 (Illustrated, forthcoming)
UFOs in America, 1947
The Watergate Affair, 1972

World War I
British Battles of World War I, 1914–15
Defeat at Gallipoli: the Dardanelles Commission Part II, 1915–16
Lord Kitchener and Winston Churchill: the Dardanelles Commission Part I, 1914–15
The Russian Revolution, 1917
War 1914: punishing the Serbs
The World War I Collection (Dardanelles Commission, British Battles of World War I)
Worldwide Battles of the Great War, 1914–1916 (Illustrated, forthcoming)

World War II
Attack on Pearl Harbor, 1941
D Day to VE Day: General Eisenhower's report, 1944–45
Escape from Germany, 1939–45
Escaping from Germany: the British government files (Illustrated, forthcoming)
The Judgment of Nuremberg, 1946
Tragedy at Bethnal Green
Victory in Europe, 1944–1945: General Eisenhower's report (Illustrated, forthcoming)
War 1939: dealing with Adolf Hitler
War in Italy, 1944: the battles for Monte Cassino (Illustrated, forthcoming)
The World War II Collection (War 1939, D Day to VE Day, Judgment of Nuremberg)

World War II facsimiles
(Illustrated books published by the British government during the war years)
The Battle of Britain, August–October 1940
The Battle of Egypt, 1942
Bomber Command, September 1939–July 1941
East of Malta, West of Suez, September 1939 to March 1941

Fleet Air Arm, 1943
The Highland Division by Eric Linklater (2004)
Land at War, 1939–1944
The Mediterranean Fleet: Greece to Tripoli (2004)
Ocean Front: the story of the war in the Pacific, 1941–1944
Roof over Britain, 1939–1942

UK Distribution and Orders
Littlehampton Book Services, Faraday Close, Durrington, West Sussex BN13 3RB
Telephone: 01903 828800 Fax: 01903 828801
E–mail: orders@lbsltd.co.uk

Sales Representation
Compass Independent Book Sales, Barley Mow Centre, 10 Barley Mow Passage,
Chiswick, London W4 4PH
Telephone: 0208 994 6477 Fax: 0208 400 6132

Other Representation
Australia
Nick Walker, Australian Book Marketing/Australian Scholarly Publishing Pty Ltd PO Box 299,
Kew, Victoria 3101; Suite 102, 282 Collins Street, Melbourne 3000 Telephone: 03 9654 0250
Fax: 03 9663 0161
E–mail: aspec@ozemail.com.au

Scandinavia
Hanne Rotovnik, Publishers' Representative, Taarbaek, PO Box 5, Strandvej 59 0,
DK–2930 Klampenborg
E–mail: Hanne@rotovnik.dk

South Africa
Colin McGee. Stephan Phillips (Pty) Ltd, PO Box 434, Umdloti Beach 4350 Telephone: +27 (0)
31 568 2902 Fax: +27 (0) 31 568 2922
E–mail: colinmcgee@mweb.co.za

All titles are available on www.amazon.com and www.amazon.co.uk.
Address distribution questions for other countries to tim.coates@yahoo.com.

www.ingramcontent.com/pod-product-compliance
Lightning Source LLC
Chambersburg PA
CBHW081134170426

43197CB00017B/2861